OBEYING EVIL

THE MOCKINGBIRD HILL MASSACRE THROUGH THE EYES OF A KILLER

RYAN GREEN

For Helen, Harvey, Frankie and Dougie

Disclaimer

This book is about real people committing real crimes. The story has been constructed by facts but some of the scenes, dialogue and characters have been fictionalised.

Polite Note to the Reader

This book is written in British English except where fidelity to other languages or accents are appropriate. Some words and phrases may differ from US English.

Copyright © Ryan Green 2017

All rights reserved

ISBN: ISBN: 154842658X
ISBN-13: 978-1548426583

YOUR FREE BOOK IS WAITING

From bestselling author Ryan Green

There is a man who is officially classed as **"Britain's most dangerous prisoner"**

The man's name is Robert Maudsley, and his crimes earned him the nickname **"Hannibal the Cannibal"**

This free book is an exploration of his story...

★★★★★ "Ryan brings the horrifying details to life. I can't wait to read more by this author!"

Get a free copy of **Robert Maudsley: Hannibal the Cannibal** when you sign up to join my Reader's Group.

www.ryangreenbooks.com/free-book

CONTENTS

Introduction 7
Part 1: The War on Chaos 12
Part 2: Mockingbird Hill 27
Part 3: Open Warfare 49
Part 4: The Last Stand 69
Part 5: Guilty as Charged 76
Part 6: Conclusion 87
Want More? 90
Every Review Helps 91
About Ryan Green 92
More Books by Ryan Green 93
Free True Crime Audiobook 97

Introduction

It was a crisp winter's morning in Arkansas. Sunlight was just starting to peek over the treetops. Behind the car, a trail of vapour streamed. The air was still, a little slice of the Peace on Earth that was the perennial promise of this season. The world was in its usual pre-Christmas lull, the dead time where nothing much happened except the building excitement of children who still thought too much of it all.

Ronald Gene Simmons, in all his years as a father, had never enjoyed it. He preferred for everything in his household to be calm. To have order. There was no order to this time of year, with people coming and going at all hours. Traitors. That was what they were. Traitors who would abandon their own flesh and blood if they were given half a chance. They were all against him. After this, there would be no more wayward sons or wayward daughters. There would be no more wayward wives for that matter. His mind slid away from thoughts of family and home. He knew the cost of distraction—you had to keep your mind on the task at hand. Not to mention the way that thoughts of them made the corners of his eyes prick and itch. He squeezed tighter on the steering wheel of the car and bit back a sob. Even his own body was trying to betray him. This was enemy territory; he couldn't afford to show weakness. Not even for a moment.

The people in the town were all against him, too. That bitch of a secretary who had cost him a good job shuffling paper around. All those liars and penny pinchers at the store who wouldn't pay him a fraction of what he was worth. He saw the way that they looked at him eyes void of respect. They thought that they could treat him like he was nothing. Like Ronald Gene Simmons wasn't a man to be reckoned with. Well, the reckoning was coming now. All the traitors were going to pay for what they had done to him. Every last person who had betrayed him was going to learn what the price of crossing a real man was.

From outside the car, the turbulence within was invisible. He drove along the Interstate to Russellville, carefully abiding by the speed limit. He slowed as he came into town, taking the time to look out along Main Street at all of the Christmas shoppers, scurrying about their business, trying to find the perfect gifts for their friends and families. Ronald already had the perfect things picked out for his children, for his wife, for the others who were coming around with them. He had given Becky permission to put up a tree without his supervision. He had given her the last of the money he had earned from odd jobs, bar the skinny bundle of bills in his wallet, to buy everyone presents, too. She should have been happy, but the more he lavished on her, the more he felt her drawing away. It wasn't Becky's fault of course. Becky was too simple to come up with anything like this for herself. Becky couldn't wash a dish without him there to hold her hand the whole way.

Becky was being led astray by the other one, by the foul temptress who was dragging them all down to Hell with her. She had been the start of it. The temptress had poisoned them all against him, sent them off wandering through the desert on their own without their father's hand to guide them. It was enough to make a grown man weep. When he pulled into the busy Walmart parking lot, Ronald had to steer around the bustle of bodies, stopping and starting, until he found a space. He sat for a time in the car with the engine still running, trying to force his white knuckles to loosen their grip on the wheel. He had to be calm. Now wasn't the time to be emotional. He knew his mission. He knew what needed to be done to complete it. Anything other than that was just going to hurt him, and he had been hurt enough for one lifetime.

He turned off the engine and hauled himself out into the cold. It wasn't a long walk. Even the biggest store in this small town didn't justify more than a few rows of parking spaces, but he had to brush past the other parents to get inside. They didn't look at him. They very deliberately didn't look at him. It was a small town, so it was no surprise that they knew him. None of them were fool enough to try greeting him, of course. Here in town he willingly suffered their stares so long as there were no whispers. Back in New Mexico, there had been whispers and worse. That was what drove him up here into the biting cold. He didn't even trouble to look at them. They had no respect, but they feared him, and that was close enough in a pinch. They wouldn't cross him if they could avoid it. Not like the traitors and the tricksters and her.

Inside the store, he practiced every courtesy that he had ever been able to fake. Smiling to the sales girl, chatting away calmly to deflect any questions, counting off the dollars and pressing them into her hand, ignoring the flinch as his dry fingertips brushed over the soft skin of her palm. Savouring that flinch, too. He took his package back to the car in a bubble of silence. The time was drawing closer now. The pieces were all in place. As it came closer and closer to the final moment, Ronald found the rest of the world falling away. There must have been more stares, carefully averted, as he walked away. There must have been more soft-faced mothers rushing to spoil their children and blank-eyed fathers rolling their eyes at every purchase, but as he walked back to the car he could not recall a single one of them. He slipped himself back behind the wheel, set his present down on the seat beside him, and carefully fastened his belt before drawing in a steadying breath.

All the false cheer and decorations might not have brought any fondness into Ronald's heart, but that little parcel beside him drew him back into happy memories. Back to that brief window, the good years, when everything made sense and people respected him. He had his medals, still squirrelled away in his room up on Mockingbird Hill, where prying eyes and thieving hands couldn't find them, but the medals didn't mean half as much as the memories. In those days, one thing followed on from the next naturally. There was no need for jarring pauses to weigh up his options. There were no fleeting ghosts. There were his orders, and there was order. He followed his own orders now, made his own rules, and followed them strictly, but it just wasn't the same. Ronald quickly double-checked his mirrors and his seatbelt then pulled away. That happened all the time now, that juddering pause as he had to stop everything and check that he was following the right routine. He knew why it happened; it was her. She would distract him if she could. She would make him forget to do the things that he needed to do. Ronald had a plan in place to take care of that little problem along with every other one. Ronald had lots of plans. It was still only barely morning and all of his errands were run. That was what order, efficiency, and planning ahead could do for your life. With a satisfied nod, he headed for the safety of home.

The bubble of silence started to fade by the time he hit the highway. When he was acting or planning, it was like a switch was flicked. He was safe from all the chaos, safe from her. But in these quiet times with nothing to do, it was all that he could do to hold back a scream. The traitors had wounded him in a way that he had never believed he could be hurt. It wasn't just that it was so unexpected; it was like they had chosen the one place where he was softest to dig in their knives. His grip tightened on the wheel again as static on the radio drowned out the Christmas carols. Ronald was surrounded by the static as he drove. That prickling chaos drowned out the whole world beyond the ragged sound of his own hot breath, the only warm thing in this godforsaken place, beading droplets on his moustache hairs.

Mockingbird Hill was up a winding dirt track off the main road, carefully fenced off from intruders and prying eyes. Ronald had to get out to move the gate aside, the cold metal sticking to his fingers. He rolled the car forward and then turned back to close up the gate behind him. Another pointless stutter. He drove on up his driveway, past the rusted carcasses of abandoned cars on either side until home reared up in front of him. Home was nothing but two mobile homes, welded together, but it was his and he was damned if anyone was going to take it away from him.

He brought the car to a halt and willed the calm to come over him again. The children were off to school. Becky would be pottering around the house, doing next to nothing as usual. He had all the time in the world. Out in the yard, he could see the turned soil of the new cesspit. In the seat beside him was his present. Everything was in place. There was no reason to feel anxious or guilty anymore. That time had passed.

Ronald unpacked his present and loaded it carefully. It was the same size as the one he had used back in the good old days to win his awards for marksmanship. It felt right in his hand. It was cool, but not cold, not like the metal outside. Even now, it warmed in his grip, becoming more alive with every moment. He drew in a shaking breath and let it out slowly. The static started to fade away. He was exactly where he needed to be. This was where his plan came together. This was when the temptress lost her grip on him, when he wrestled free of her, when he set his family free. With the gun in his hand, he stepped out into the chill morning air and drew it all in. It was steady now. There was no more time for doubt or fear. No more time for chaos. This was his time. This was the order that he was going to instil in the world. He strode across his yard and drew the sliding door open gently.

Part 1: The War on Chaos

It is grimly appropriate that Ronald Gene Simmons' story does not properly start with his birth, but with a death. While he was born on a hot summer's day in Chicago, Illinois, in 1940, it was a little under three years later that his world began to spin off its axis, starting him down the path that would lead him to his defining moments. Details about Loretta and William Simmons have mostly faded from history. In light of their son's infamy, the family has become reluctant to discuss them with outsiders, but it seems that for those first three years Ronald lived as normal a life as any other baby might. But in January of 1943, chaos arrived into Ronald's life for the very first time, striking down his father with a lethal stroke. The bubble of familiarity and safety surrounding Ronald popped in an instant. One of the two most important figures in his life vanished in an instant, for no apparent reason beyond the obscene fact that sometimes people just die.

Along with William, the economic stability of regular income also vanished. Loretta had lived through the Great Depression. She could remember all too keenly what hunger and desperation felt like. The 40s were not a time when a single woman could easily make a life for herself and an orphaned boy, so she worked quickly using the only means that were at her disposal to secure her future and that of her toddler, Ronald. By the end of the year, she was remarried.

If that had been the only moment of instability, then it is possible that Ronald could have recovered his sense of balance and order, but his new stepfather, William D. Griffen, served in the US Army Corps of Engineers. The family moved to Arkansas when Griffen was deployed there, then they moved again, and again, and again. For ten years the family, was in a state of constant flux, never settling for long in one place.

The disruption had a marked effect on Ronald. He was always the new kid at every school he attended, never staying in one place for long enough to make any friends, and showing a stark lack of the social skills that would have been required to make friends anyway. Ronald quickly developed a reputation as a troublemaker and a bully. He struggled with his schoolwork and lashed out at his classmates with little provocation.

If he had stayed in one place for long enough, it is possible that his teachers might have found the underlying cause of this behaviour and helped him to adapt, but anything resembling stability eluded him until he was sixteen years old. By that time, his violent outbursts had progressed to the point that even the school system of the 50s couldn't go on considering his behaviour to be 'boys being boys.' Having rapidly blown through their entire arsenal of disciplinary tools, the school was left with no option but except to expel Ronald. In a last ditch attempt to punish the boy into good behaviour, his parents shipped him off to military school, where they hoped that martial discipline might finally bring him to his senses.

To everyone's amazement, including Ronald's, military school had the desired effect. He didn't break under the strict order and pressure of the school's rigorous routines. He thrived. As the boys around him had their spirits crushed by the relentless routine of military school, Ronald found a sense of peace and purpose that he had been lacking his entire life.

Within the military structure, his aggressive impulses were turned to constructive goals, and his desire for complete control of the world around him was mirrored in his environment for the first time. He rose before the sun, went through a routine of preparing his clothes and bunk for inspection, showering, exercising, marching and drilling. Every moment of his day was filled; every moment of his day was ordered. When his time at the military school came to its end, he was unwilling to leave and return to his civilian life outside of that safe cocoon of order. He dropped out of high school at the age of 17, severed ties to his family, and joined the Navy as quickly as possible.

His first posting was Bremerton Naval Base in Washington, where he met a young woman by the name of Bersabe Rebecca Ulibarri. Becky, as she was known, was considered to be the local beauty, her long black hair was the envy of all the local girls. Expectations were high for her. Their courtship was slow in the beginning, but unwavering. With the disciplined structure of the Navy behind him, Ronald was calm enough to express himself with some degree of charisma, and he won Becky over. The couple began living together, which was when Becky first caught a glimpse of Ronald's dark side and the shape that the rest of her life was going to take.

*

The bowl shook in Becky's hand when she heard the door slam, but she wrote off the nervous flinch as a sign of excitement. Ronald was home. What did she have to be unhappy about? She turned to greet him with a smile. Ronald had never been one for smiling, but he gave her the firm nod that usually served as a greeting between them. He sat down at the kitchen table and lit a cigarette without saying a word. Becky didn't mind some companionable silence. They were comfortable together, that was all. Not every minute of the day had to be filled up with chatter. She turned back to the sink and started over on the bowl. She could feel his gaze on her. The intensity of it had been half of the draw of Ronald when they first met. You could tell just by meeting his eyes that he had some passion in him. The boys that she had considered dating before Ronald had been just that, boys. Ronald was every inch a man, and if that meant that he was a little stern sometimes, well that was just a part of his charm.

She lifted the bowl out of the water and set it aside before turning her attention to the pots. They had already been washed once, but now she was rinsing them off so that there was no residue. Ronald was very particular about how things were done around the house, and there was nothing wrong with that either. It was nice to meet a man who was house proud instead of slovenly. If it meant that he was unhappy with her once in a while, then that was her failing, not his. If she could just do things the way that they were meant to be done, he wouldn't have to scold her. Some days, she could swear that she was doing exactly the same as the last, but somehow her work was always slipping below his standards. He had the patience of a saint. Becky knew that most men wouldn't treat her so gently when she kept on making mistakes all of the time. Ronald had never raised a hand to her, just his voice, and barely even that. She knew how lucky she was. Don't let anybody ever say that she wasn't lucky to have found a man as kind and caring as Ronald.

When she lifted the pot out from the clear water she caught a glimpse of a stranger reflected back in the stainless steel. The girl who she used to be had vanished. She was growing up, and the way that she dressed and the way that she behaved had to reflect that. Having hair all over the place was fine when you were out courting, but now that she was settled down it was time to bring her jezebel locks under control. Her hair had been her pride and joy, but pride was a sin, and with his gentle words, Ronald had helped her purge herself of that sin. It wasn't lopped off or anything so drastic. It was just pulled back from her face and tied away modestly. She still had her beauty, but it wasn't something to be flashed at any man who walked by the window. It was for her husband to be. The face beneath the hair was much changed, too. The makeup that she had once laboured over for hours was gone, long gone. Ronald couldn't abide vanity, but in his soft whispers, he appealed to hers inadvertently, telling her that she was beautiful without all that makeup, that other girls might need it, but not her. If it made Ronald happy and it was a lot less work for her, then whom did it hurt if she just did what he wanted? Her clothes had to change, but that was just being practical. She wore her button-down shirts with pride. They may not have been as fancy as the clothes that she wore when she was younger, but she wasn't some young thing out on the prowl now—she was a settled woman. Ronald had to wear his uniform every day to do his service to the country, so how was it any different when she put on hers?

She was distracted in that moment. She didn't hear him get up. She just felt the warm presence behind her like a weight on her back. She startled and almost dropped the pot. It would land in the sink and soak her, soak the countertops that she had spent exactly twenty minutes polishing to perfection. The water might even get on Ronald, and that wouldn't do. He caught the pot before it had even left her fingers. His arms wrapped around her. He stepped in close and took hold of her hands, guiding the washcloth over the pot in one smooth movement that lifted all of the last traces of soap away. She felt his voice vibrating in his chest as much as she heard him speaking softly in her ear, 'Careful there, my clumsy girl. That is the way to do it. You're getting the hang of it. Now do the rest again. Just like that.'

He drew away from her just as suddenly as he had appeared. Returning to his cigarette still burning in the ashtray. The ashtray. She had forgotten to clean out the ashtray. It was one of the first jobs that she usually did in the morning after Ronald left for work. How could she have been so stupid? He must have been sitting there, looking at the ashtray overflowing with muck and holding back a scream. How could she have let him down like that? She dumped the pot onto the clean pile, lifted the rest of them back onto the other side and dried off her hands on the dishtowel. He didn't even look up when she came over to empty it, but when she reached out he caught her wrist in his hand with almost casual ease. He grunted, 'It will keep until I'm done. Just finish the pots.'

Becky was frozen for a moment, torn between gratitude that he was being so forgiving, dread that his anger was going to fall on her later when she wasn't braced for it, and confusion. She had thought that he would have lost his temper, but he didn't even seem to care today. Had she completely misunderstood why he was angry at her the last time that the ashtray hadn't been emptied? Had she been imagining a foul temper for this sweet and loving man? He drew on his cigarette and smiled up at her, one of those rare glimpses of kindness on his face to match the kindness she knew was in his heart to put up with a girl like her. He let her wrist slip out of his grasp, and if it felt a little sore or a little bruised, that was just because he was a big strong man as well as a kind one. She turned back to her duties.

*

When Ronald was redeployed to New Mexico, Becky followed, and they were married a few days before his twentieth birthday. If Becky thought that he was controlling before they were married, the new commitment only seemed to increase his drive to dominate her. Before the move to New Mexico, he had already begun dictating what clothes she was allowed to wear, how she wore her hair and limiting the time she spent with her friends.

It seemed that Ronald had no real sense of loyalty or love, and couldn't understand those drives in others. He believed that if Becky remained as beautiful as she was when he first met her, then other men would begin courting her and attract her attention. He could not tolerate abandonment. He stripped her of her carefully crafted appearance and broke down her confidence in herself with a steady grind of corrections and complaints until she was convinced that she could do nothing on her own and had to rely on him for everything.

Once they made the move to New Mexico, he severed all ties with her family. Becky no longer received her own mail, and all attempts to contact her through Ronald were stilted at best and ignored at worst. Every moment of her life was scheduled around fulfilling Ronald's needs. With a normal man, this would have been intolerable, but with a man whose needs included complete control over everything around him, it was a living nightmare—one that he successfully convinced Becky she deserved due to her own incompetence. For the following few years, their marriage remained in a state of painful equilibrium. Becky would do everything and anything that was asked of her, up to and including being a verbal punching bag whenever Ronald's foul moods required it.

Only a year into the marriage, Becky gave birth to their first child, Ronald Gene Simmons, Junior, who later went by Gene. Two years after that, just as Ronald's abusive behaviour began to spike following his discharge from the Navy, a second child was born, Sheila Marie Simmons, who rapidly became the apple of his eye.

His controlling behaviour worsened in the years after he left the Navy, but returned to normal levels a couple of years later after he signed up with the Air Force and returned to a life of discipline and order. During those two years, his demands became less like those of a dictator and more like those of a pesky office manager, hovering over Becky as she completed every task in her day, preventing her from going outside unaccompanied and gradually crushing every last moment of freedom out of his carefully planned schedule for her. If Becky realised that her situation was worsening, then she did very little about it, going along with whatever Ronald wanted.

Over the following years, he would father five more children with Becky: William, Loretta, Eddie, Marianne, and Rebecca Lyn. Each child was quickly allotted tasks and a position within the order he was creating in his household. To outsiders, they would appear to be little more than household chores, albeit chores that were more difficult than you might expect children so young to undertake, but the truth was more insidious. Ronald could not tolerate free agents under his roof. If the children could not be trusted to obey him in all things, then they could not stay. The blocks of work that he assigned to them were as much a test of their loyalty as a part of his pathological desire to control others.

Ronald took to spending his free time with Sheila more and more often as the years rolled on. By the time she turned thirteen, his affection had grown to the point that others began to take note. His other children were objects to be manipulated, pieces of the puzzle of chaotic life that he had to slot together in such a way as to give the appearance of order. But in Sheila, he seemed to believe that he had found some sort of kindred spirit. She received all of the favours that the grim-faced man ever dispensed to his children. Of all the people in his life, the only one who you would ever suspect Ronald Gene Simmons ever truly loved was Sheila. On one of the few family occasions that Ronald could not avoid, his whole family went to visit his sister-in-law for Christmas. Sheila would have been about fifteen years old at the time. The behaviour that the rest of his immediate, well-trained family believed was perfectly normal made Becky's sister incredibly uncomfortable. Sheila came over to the seat where Ronald was scowling at the room and draped herself over his lap as though she were a toddler rather than a girl well on her way to womanhood. When even that wasn't enough to break him out of his characteristic foul mood, she leaned in and gave him a kiss, not on the cheek as a daughter would, but on the lips. The rest of Ronald's children and even Becky didn't bat an eye. This was just how the two of them behaved together.

*

For all of his problems with impulse control and manipulative behaviour, you might have expected Ronald to do badly in a career that requires discipline and loyalty, but for the 22 years that he served in the United States Military, it would seem that he was an exemplary officer, finally retiring at the rank of Master Sergeant in 1979. During his service, he had not only earned the respect of his comrades, he had also acquired a Bronze Star, The Republic of Vietnam Cross, and the Air Force Ribbon. During his service, he also received numerous rewards for his marksmanship, in particular with the .22 calibre pistol, his weapon of choice. As a decorated veteran, he retired with all due honours to their rented home in Cloudcroft, New Mexico.

The tension in that house must have been palpable on Ronald's last day of work. While the children would not have been old enough to remember the nightmarish lockdown that followed Ronald's last brief retirement, their mother must have known all too well just how bad things were about to get, even if she would never acknowledge it out loud. Imagine her surprise when Ronald came home and, instead of the furious, controlling monster that she expected, she was greeted by her husband as if it were a normal day. Sheila bounced over to give her father a kiss and his face cracked into a genuine smile. It seemed like things were going to be all right for all of them.

Grocery shopping was the most exciting part of Becky's week. Ronald hadn't tightened his grip on her quite so firmly this time. She was allowed out into town on her own, but she knew that it irritated him when she was out and about when he needed her for something. Irritating Ronald was a bad idea. When he announced that he would drive her to the store, it was almost a relief. If he was coming into town with her, then she at least knew that he wasn't alone at home, getting riled up over some mistake that she had made. She dashed about the house, finishing up the last of her chores as well as she could, then grabbed her coat and headed out to the car. Ronald was already inside, the engine was already on, and she could faintly make out the sound of music playing on the radio. Ronald had a smile plastered on his face and was nodding along to the music as if he had a single musical bone in his body. Becky couldn't help but smile herself. He hadn't always been like this. She could still remember when they were first courting, how much fun they had together. For a dreadful moment, a spark of hope warmed her chest. If he had been happy with her before, then he could be happy with her again. This retirement could be a chance for them to find that happiness together again. She would stop making so many foolish mistakes and he would learn to smile again.

With a bounce in her step for the first time in two decades, Becky walked around the back of the car, smiling down at her own feet, almost bashful to be getting into the car with this strange man. When she got to the passenger's side door, she saw what he was smiling about. Sheila was sitting there, in her seat, with a big grin on her face. Becky could see the laughter on her face, saw her mouthing the word, 'Daddy!' as she slapped playfully at his shoulder. Becky's stomach dropped as she pulled the door open. Sheila was already strapped in and ready to go. The smile vanished from Ronald's face the moment he saw her. He nodded to the back seats.

Becky opened her mouth to complain, to argue, to fight back against this latest indignity in a gruelling lifetime of them. She saw Ronald's eyes, just waiting for her to try it. She shut the door and climbed into the back seat without a word. Her cheeks burned with shame as they pulled out of the driveway. Relegated to the back seat like she was the child and Sheila was his wife. She looked at Sheila, still giggling and happy, unaware that she was pushing her mother out with every kind word and smile. Never even realising the knife that she was twisting in her mother's back with every kindness that Ronald bestowed on her. His perfect little girl.

Becky had never been perfect. She tried and she tried to please Ronald, but his standards always seemed to be just out of reach. He looked at her with sympathy more than affection after all of these years. Whatever love he might have felt had been eroded by the daily disappointments of living with her. He used to look at her like that. That was the worst part about it—not the shame or the indignity, but remembering a time when he loved her, when he took the time to guide her hands as she went through her chores. When he took the time to tell her what he needed instead of glowering at her with barely restrained resentment. She knew that she had been letting him down, but she had never suspected that his love would be diverted to a more deserving vessel. Between the front seats, Becky watched their hands clasp together. Father and daughter, bound together in love. She never knew that she could feel jealousy towards her own daughter, that it could burn like this, as deep in her gut as the coil of embarrassment as the neighbours saw them driving by. When they arrived at the grocery store, Ronald gave no indication that he had any intention of getting out. Sheila was so lost in conversation with her father that she didn't even seem to have recognised that they had arrived. Eventually, she caught Ronald's eyes in the rear-view mirror. His brows drew down and he grumbled, 'Go on then. We'll be waiting for you.'

Like a stranger in her own marriage, Becky climbed out of the car and walked into the grocery store. She felt numb. She hadn't been rejected so much as she had been casually dismissed. She paused in the doorway before the hum of the air conditioner drowned out all of the sound from outside and glanced back at the car with her husband and daughter inside. Sheila was leaning over to kiss her father, missing his cheek entirely and planting her lips firmly on his in the midst of the beard that he had just begun to grow. They still hadn't broken apart by the time that Becky turned away and started her drudge around the shelves.

As with every other discomfort that Ronald's demands and control over her caused, Becky was expected to bear her gradual replacement in his affections with silence. If he had been conducting an affair in private, far from the public eye, then she could have borne it with some dignity. Instead, she was brought into a family meeting where Ronald laid out the facts of his relationship with Sheila in the most brutal way possible. At seventeen-years-old, Sheila was pregnant with his child. He intended for her to have the child, and to raise it as a part of the family. He intended to continue his incestuous relationship with her openly and he wanted the family to support him. This was the breaking point. The moment where any sane person would bring the whole twisted structure that Ronald had been building all of these years crashing down. But it wasn't Becky who broke. Disgusted and ashamed, she was still too thoroughly in Ronald's power to ever go against him. She gave in, rolled over and submitted, just as he had expected her to. Rebellion instead came from an unexpected source.

After a lifetime of watching his mother ground under his father's heel, Ronald Gene Simmons, Junior, had seen enough. Gene had spent every waking moment receiving the same soul crushing treatment as his siblings, so he did not dare to confront his father directly, but he had options. He firmly believed that talking directly with the police would be useless. After all, if the authorities had been too blind to notice the constant abuse all of these years, why would they suddenly change their opinion now. He came at the problem laterally, through one of the only channels where he could expect to find empathy rather than a carbon copy of his father in a different uniform. He reported Sheila's pregnancy anonymously to her school counsellor.

Over the course of many meetings, starting with the first in which Sheila failed to deny that she was pregnant, her guidance counsellor worked on her to get information about the father of the child. While she was 17 years old, and thus over the age of consent in New Mexico, Sheila had never had a boyfriend in all of her high school life, and the anonymous tip had set alarm bells ringing. After almost a month, she finally broke down and admitted that the father of her child was her own father, Ronald.

Criminal charges were filed almost immediately, but Sheila outright refused to testify about the identity of her child's father. The logic that she used to justify this decision will always elude us. Some of it may have been the obvious shame and stigma that was attached to incest. Even as a victim rather than a willing participant, she would have been marked for life as a sexual deviant. We also know that the emotional bombardment from her father was reaching a fever pitch during her days in court. Rather than trying to cajole and calm her, he instead went on the offensive. Blaming her for bringing the family into disrepute, blaming her for trying to ruin his life and destroy the happiness that they had found together. In a surviving letter from this time, there is another chilling turn of phrase. Ronald wrote, 'You have destroyed me and you have destroyed my trust in you. I will see you in hell.'

It is unclear exactly what was happening within the family at this time, because they closed ranks. The children had previously been allowed friends and visitors, provided they gave Ronald enough notice so that he could withdraw to a dark room and drink until they left, but now all connections to the community in Cloudcroft were severed. It seems fair to assume that Sheila was separated from Ronald during this period and he was prevented from seeing her in person, explaining his letters. Around this time Becky made one of her first serious attempts to leave Ronald, when the public spectacle of his behaviour finally started to outweigh her fear of him and her conviction that she was incapable of life without him.

If Ronald's proclamations of love towards Sheila had been true, then it is unlikely that fury would have been his first response. She was already actively resisting the investigation to the best of her abilities, but the fact that she had ever admitted to his molestation, even outside of an official setting, was enough to launch him into a terrible rage. As with all other things in his life, it was the loss of control that was at the root of his misery. It is possible that he felt some romantic inclination in his life, but if he did, it had no impact on his behaviour. His relationship with Sheila had nothing to do with love and everything to do with power and domination, like most acts of incest. With the other members of his family, Ronald found some degree of calm merely by controlling their actions, but when it came to his favourite child, Sheila, just controlling her every waking moment was insufficient. He had to own every part of her, including her body. She may have benefitted from the arrangement as he framed his obsession as lavishing extra attention on her, but ultimately her happiness was never relevant to him, and he took far more than he gave. If Sheila had not become the target of his need for control, then any of his other children could have become his victim. If Sheila had not responded to his advances in the way that he desired, then it is likely that he would have moved on to one of the younger girls, as that seemed to be the direction that his sexual proclivities leaned.

Over the course of his life, Ronald seems to have treated all women who he met in a similar manner. To his mind, they existed solely as outlets for his desires, and minor details such as their interest in him and the fact that they were members of his family could be ignored if it meant getting what he wanted.

Impregnating Sheila was the logical conclusion to his domination. He not only owned every part of her but had transformed her from a young girl into a vessel for him. She was no longer allowed to exist as a person; she was only a repository for his dark passions. With Becky, the pleasure that he took in impregnation seemed to have passed all too quickly, explaining the sheer number of children that he forced her to carry. With Sheila, that pleasure was more complete. Not only was she forced to carry a child that it is fair to assume that she did not want, she was also trapped within a crushing web of guilt and shame. Just when his pleasure in total control over Sheila was approaching its natural conclusion, it was spoiled by the intrusion of the outside world, the world that he couldn't control.

The family began to fragment. Gene, already desperate to get away from his father and seizing on this moment of weakness, left to start a life of his own. Without Ronald's constant looming presence, the ridiculousness of the other children's slavish obedience became increasingly apparent to them, and in his depressive state, he rarely even bothered to chastise them for ignoring the routines that he had laid out for them. Without constant reinforcement, the discipline that Ronald had spent their entire lives trying to enforce began to fall apart until he realised that his situation was untenable.

Despite Sheila's stonewalling of the investigation and refusal from all parties to testify, the charges of incest were still making their gradual way through the legal system of New Mexico. For the first time in his adult life, the chaos of the outside world was once again intruding on the stability that Ronald had managed to construct for himself. His response was predictably explosive. He uprooted the entire family and fled the state. The rented house where he had been lurking since he left the armed forces was found abandoned. Without ceremony, the Simmons family vanished.

Part 2: Mockingbird Hill

Almost an entire year passed with no sign of the family. Sheila's due date passed by with it, and the investigation into Ronald Gene Simmons ground slowly to a halt in the absence of either the perpetrator or the victim of the crime. Eventually, the courts in Cloudcroft gave up entirely, filing the investigation into Sheila's pregnancy away with all of the other cold cases. In the 80s, jurisdictional conflicts and poor communication made escapes like this all too simple and all too common. Many serial killers escaped notice in the same manner, skipping between states to avoid attention. The legal apparatus of the time simply wasn't equipped to pursue criminals beyond state borders, and the consensus at the time was that 'non-violent' crimes like the one that Ronald had committed on his daughter were not to be given priority.

In Ward, Arkansas, the family settled into a hermetic life for two years, with as little contact with the outside world as it was possible to have. If Ronald worked during this time, he was paid under the table. If they rented property during this time, it is safe to assume that it was paid for in cash, or that rent simply went unpaid as the Simmonses bounced from one property to the next. The absolute chaos of a life without any time to lay down roots, the same situation that drove Ronald to the verge of madness in his adolescence, had returned with a vengeance. Still reeling from what he perceived as a betrayal at the hands of his daughter, Ronald turned inward while still lashing out brutally at his family. Within two years, any hope of escape that they might have been harbouring after that brief glimpse of freedom had faded. When Ronald uprooted them again, there was no sense of relief that life was going to fall back into place, just the continual dread that came with sharing space with a man with no care for anything but his own control.

Fifteen miles outside of Dover, Arkansas, the Simmons family finally found their new home. Mockingbird Hill was a fanciful name for what was essentially an abandoned lot. To reach the 'house' you had to drive up a long winding driveway of rutted red clay in a heavily wooded area, practically impassable in the heavy rain or snow that was typical for the area. Once you had passed the dozens of 'No Trespassing' signs that dotted the path, the structure itself came into sight. The 'house' was comprised of two aging mobile homes that had been welded together haphazardly into a single larger structure.

After the chaotic period of their escape and cross-country flight, several of the older children were beginning to rail against Ronald's control. Gene had already left the family before they took flight, and some of the older children, Sheila included, were now beginning to seriously question whether they wanted to spend any more time in their father's tender care. If there had never been any outside interference, then Ronald would never have shown weakness, but now that the family was coming to realise that he was not as all-powerful as he once appeared, the seeds of rebellion had been planted. Ronald responded in the only way that he knew how—he tried to tighten his grip on them.

*

Little Becky started to cry early on. Her mother wouldn't come out of the kitchen. She had sat herself down at the dining table and started to smoke after serving Daddy his breakfast and she hadn't moved since. She wouldn't look out through the plate glass doors no matter how the children cried. You could see her flinch every time one of her children shrieked, but she didn't dare to move. She didn't dare to fight for them. The older ones had already learned that sobs were just going to earn them a scowl from Daddy. They didn't even bother anymore, not for something as small as pain. If it caught them by surprise—if they lost their grip on a cinderblock and it landed on their foot, or if a corner caught on one of the blisters on their hands—then they might let out a little gasp or a little yelp, but it would be by reflex. They marched back and forth in a line, from the pile of rubble that Daddy had found on the property when he was deciding where the grass needed cut, to the new wall. It crept up, row by row, around the front of the property, slowly blocking off any sight of the house from the outside world.

Little Becky was only eight years old. The blocks that weighed her brothers and sisters down made her shoulders strain and pop in their sockets. The others had blisters, but their hands were hardened by years of chores. Hers just bled. Every block that Little Becky slotted into the wall was marked red at the corners. She would have gone begging to Daddy for a job that didn't hurt her so much if she thought that it would do any good, but he wouldn't trust her with the work that he was doing around the back of the yard. The front wall would rise up taller than the one at the back. The lines of trees at the back bordered on some neighbour's property. Once or twice since they had arrived, Little Becky and the others had perked up at the sound of other children playing outside. They had even caught glimpses of them through the woods. Daddy wasn't going to stand for strangers wandering into his yard any more than he would trust any one of his kids to talk to a neighbour. The only reason that the cinderblock wall at the back of the property was shorter was so that he could coil barbed wire all along the top of it without needing a ladder. Eddy and Loretta had to help him with that, and both of them had come to bed that night with iodine stained hands all scratched to pieces. The only one who was safe from the wall was Barbara. She was confined to her room with the hope that if Daddy didn't see her, then he wouldn't give her work to do.

They had been here for three days now, since Daddy had got the keys from the town down below. Every morning he had woken them up at dawn with a different chore to do that day. On the first night, before they even hauled the boxes in from the car, the oldest ones had to dig a cesspit because the new house didn't have a toilet. Daddy didn't mind. He said it reminded him of his army days. Every day since then they had been working on these projects. Cutting back the long grass all over the yard. Setting up a chicken coop. Gathering up Daddy's bottles from where he tossed them around the yard. Getting a doghouse knocked together for Bo and Duke so that they didn't have to sleep in the house, whining and hollering all night long. Stacking up any of the 'building materials' into heaps to be used later. Plotting out spots for the next few months' cesspits. The wall was just the latest in a long list.

The brick slipped from between Little Becky's aching fingers and left a scratch down the length of her leg before clipping off the side of her heel. She tried to hold it in but the tears started running down her cheeks anyway. She didn't cry out, but she shook. The forest blurred as she fumbled, trying to get a new grip on the cinderblock despite her quaking hands. She didn't know who it was, but suddenly there were arms wrapped around her, holding her in a tight circle of warmth. She could smell the sweet tang of sweat, a faint hint of her mother's perfume and the cloying damp that hung on all of their clothes after weeks of living in a car. Whoever it was only held on for a moment before breaking away. Just long enough for her to catch her breath but not long enough to catch Daddy's attention. Blood was staining her sock when she looked down, but it hardly mattered. There was already a little bloody smear on her skirt. There were rusty marks and grass stains on her sneakers too. She would already be punished for messing up her clothes if Daddy decided that punishment was in order. One more mark didn't matter.

With the strength that her brother or sister's hug had imparted, Little Becky got her fingers curled under the corners of the cinderblock and hefted it back up again. The muscles of her back, her shoulders, and her arms all stretched to their limit then vibrated like a guitar string being plucked. Her hands went on shaking, but her grip was true despite the morning dew that the cinderblock had picked up. She carried on her march towards the wall before Daddy could notice her slacking. Building the walls of her own prison.

Over the course of several weeks, Ronald fortified Mockingbird Hill in such a way that any potential visitors would be dissuaded and any hopeful peeping toms would find their hobby impossible. If the isolated location and dense forest surrounding the property weren't enough, the threatening trespasser warning signs and the walls and barbed wire that he forced his children to lay out around the property were probably enough to ensure that there wouldn't be many visitors.

Ronald had learned his lesson about allowing the outside world to see what life inside his little kingdom was really like. If absolute isolation was required to maintain absolute control, then he would create it. He had never particularly cared for the company of others anyway. In addition to learning how secretive he needed to be, he also learned the value of maintaining his family's anonymity by carefully following the rules. His children had perfect attendance at their schools, and while they had some trouble socialising, as they were on strict schedules that allowed no time for friendships outside of the classroom, none of them struggled academically. They remained in the middle of the pack throughout their entire school life in Arkansas, never drawing any attention to themselves or their unusual home life.

A new stress appeared in Ronald's life about this time. When he uprooted his family and severed all ties to his past in New Mexico, he also lost access to the generous pensions that he had accrued from his time in military service. For his entire adult life, money had never been a pressing concern for him. He was cared for by the military during his service and after retiring as a master sergeant. His pension had been sufficient to cover rent and bills. Without that money, he was forced to seek out employment. Even in the best circumstances, jobs were difficult to find in rural Arkansas. The town of Dover had a population of only a few hundred families, but that limited population required very little infrastructure to support it. Small towns without local industry subsist in tiny, mostly sealed economies, where money is just shuffled around between the local residents, with a small amount coming in from exports and considerably more being siphoned out when they have to import goods. To get a job within a small town, you need one of two things: a unique and highly valuable skill or a family member with some influence. As an outsider with no experience outside of the military, Ronald had no opportunities at all in Dover, and like most people seeking work outside of the comfort of the city, he was forced to travel 30 miles to nearby Russellville to find even the lowest paying work.

In a very real way, this was the first time that Ronald had to deal with regular working life outside of the comfortable structure of the military, and he took to it very poorly. After a lifetime of receiving high praise for the quality of his work and receiving literal medals for doing his job correctly, he felt like the paltry salary that he could now command massively undervalued him. In his military life, he had acquired a position of command and earned the respect of his peers. While there were people of a higher rank who he had to interact with as part of his work, he'd never had to deal with the American people before. He was overwhelmed by the constant disrespect that he received from employers, co-workers, and the general public. For a normal veteran, it would have been difficult, but for an egomaniac like Ronald, every day became a constant war with those around him as imagined slights blossomed into vendettas in his mind. As with everything else that caused him discomfort, Ronald struggled in a situation that he could not completely control and that he did not understand the underlying rules of. In the military, there was a chain of command that could be easily followed. He had to obey the orders of anyone of a higher rank because that was the nature of military life, but in civilian jobs, anyone and everyone could place pressures on him, and he had no way of knowing which demands needed to be obeyed and which could be ignored.

And then there was the problem with Ronald's continuing attitude towards women as nothing more than objects for his sexual appetites.

Despite the steep odds, Ronald secured a good position in a law firm as a clerk almost immediately after arrival in Russellville, a role in which his natural proclivity for organisation and his anal attention to detail were actually assets rather than hindrances. All reports on the quality and speed of his work showed that he was an intelligent and diligent worker. The same traits that had made him a success in the military were producing positive results in his civilian life for the first time. Sadly, the diligence and competence that he carried on with him were not accompanied by any structures of discipline.

While the military had always kept Ronald on a short leash, there was nobody to hold him back now. There was nobody with the power to stop him from behaving in what he seemed to think was a normal manner, replicating his home life down at the office. There were few women in the office, but like at home, he chose one younger woman to be the focus of his attentions. Unlike with Sheila at home, his target, Kathy Kendricks, had spent some time socialising outside of a twisted family setting. She was able to recognise the grossly inappropriate sexual advances that he was making towards her as abusive rather than flattering. He had nothing to offer a partner. His instability was becoming ever more apparent since his loss of control back in Cloudcroft, manifesting itself as a foul temper and borderline paranoia. She reported his repeated lewd comments, and after she described Ronald's 'flirtations', which bordered on sexual assault, to her employers, he was fired promptly.

The family thought that they had seen fury before, when all of the slights against him had only been imagined. Now, he had the insult of rejection from a woman who he believed should have been his by right, little more than another piece of property, and the injury of losing the only steady work that he had managed to secure since leaving the military. The wages of a legal clerk in the 80s were nothing lavish, but they had been enough to cover the rent for his little enclave out on Mockingbird Hill, pay for groceries, and allow Ronald to anaesthetise himself with alcohol when troubling thoughts about all of those who had wronged him threatened to rear their ugly heads.

It remains unknown exactly how violent Ronald was with his wife and children. It seems obvious in hindsight that he was a violent man, so it is difficult to imagine that he never inflicted harm on them during his long campaigns of control and terror. If Ronald followed the pattern of behaviour that we see frequently among other psychopaths and abusers, this was likely to be a time of particular suffering for his children and wife as he lashed out at them as a means of letting off steam. While his wife was entirely isolated during this time, thanks to her inability to drive and the rural location, the children were never reported to be showing any signs of physical abuse, so it is entirely possible that he focused all of his violent attentions on her.

Becky had again become a sexual outlet for him after Sheila's withdrawal, perhaps expecting a similar improvement in treatment as her daughter had experienced during her time as the focus of Ronald's attentions. During the period when he was obsessing over Kathy Kendricks, it is likely that his affections were withdrawn from her all over again. Some combination of the new foul temper and the absence of anything that could be interpreted as affection was enough to push her over the edge. Becky tried to leave.

Her attempt at escape seems to have been ill conceived and short lived. Ronald had been conditioning her for decades to believe that she could not survive out in the world without him to care for her, something that she believed until her very final moments. In this first attempt, it seems just as likely that she came back home of her own volition as that he somehow coerced her. The fact that her many children were still trapped alone in a house with a man who had shown no hesitation to abuse them in the most appalling ways was probably a contributing factor in her decision to return, too. Ronald did not seem to repay this betrayal with anything more than contempt. If looked at through the warped lens of their relationship, you might take this lack of vengeance to be a kindness, but Ronald was not the kind of man to forgive and forget. This insult, along with all of the others, he filed away mentally. For now, he had more pressing concerns.

Despite the speed at which gossip must have spread in the small town of Russellville, it took Ronald only a few weeks to secure another position for himself, this time with the local oil company. While they had heard about his unpleasant reputation through the grapevine, his competence seemed undeniable, and some ingrained misogyny allowed them to discount Kendricks' complaints against him as a romance gone wrong rather than the predatory actions of a sick man. He was not able to hold the position for long before his constant insubordination and arguments with his employer, along with the first hints of unseemly behaviour towards his female co-workers, had him on the hunt for a job once more.

We don't know if Becky made her second attempt at leaving during this window of unemployment, but tracing the patterns of Ronald's domineering behaviour, it's possible. We know that Becky made several attempts to break away from Ronald during these years. The incident in Cloudcroft and the long period of chaos that followed had clearly shaken her faith in what must have seemed a near-godlike ability to predict and control all of the elements in his life.

With their newfound sense of security, the children were settling comfortably into new schools, quickly catching up on the work that they had missed and resuming their positions in the middle of the pack. Also, with Ronald now frequently out of the house at work, they began to develop social lives without his constant interference. The younger children made friends for the first time. The older children could now make evening trips into the nearby towns, where most teenage matchmaking took place, for the first time. None of the children were ever so foolish as to bring a friend home to Mockingbird Hill. Despite Ronald's downward spiral, his intellect remained as sharp as ever and his paranoia had certainly not waned. Any evidence of outside interference within his domain would have resulted in a massive tantrum and an ultimately futile attempt to crack down on his rebellious children.

Following his firing at the oil company, it took Ronald a little longer to find another job. But eventually, Russellville once again proved accommodating. It seemed that patriotism was a contributing factor to his landing so many comfortable jobs. In the post-Vietnam era, there was a lot of sympathy towards veterans who were having trouble adjusting to civilian life, and most of his eccentricities were written off as shell shock. He took a new position as a clerk at the Woodline Motor Freight Company. Ronald's twisted attitude towards women had cost him two jobs in Russellville so far, and he had no intention of losing a third in the same way. Psychopaths may not be capable of changing their core behaviours, but they are absolute experts at disguising them. None of the female staff in the freight company ever had cause to complain about his inappropriate advances. In fact, he seemed to get on rather well with his co-workers, indulging in small talk and blending in with the other employees, up to a point. Ronald still harboured all of his instinctive misogyny, and he still had massive problems dealing with any sort of civilian authority. These two issues came to vex him simultaneously in the person of Joyce Elaine Butts, his new supervisor.

To say that Ronald and Joyce did not get along would be something of an understatement. He could not comprehend a world in which a woman was his superior, and she could not deal with an employee who completely ignored her very basic requests. Ronald frequently went over her head to the owner of the company whenever they were in even minor disputes, and the constant irritation of an insubordinate entry-level clerk soon outweighed any benefits that his marked competence in the role might have granted the company. On top of this, Joyce constantly admonished Ronald when it was discovered that he had resumed his attempts at courting Kathy Kendricks, showing up at her house with flowers and sending her little notes in an attempt to gain her forgiveness and favour despite the almost 30-year age gap. When he was let go, it was without any recriminations from the company, but it seemed obvious to Ronald that he had lost this latest job thanks to some sort of conspiracy between the women of Arkansas to do harm to him.

At some point, Ronald became aware that his children had cultivated social lives, but by this time he was so caught up in his paranoid vendettas that he could not spare the energy to intervene. At the same time, it is possible that he recognised any further attempts to block his children from interacting with society was going to draw unwanted attention to them. After all, it was already widely commented on by the children's friends that they were never allowed to visit the Simmons' home. When it came to his attention that one of the older boys, Billy, was not only dating but was seriously considering settling down with a girl, Ronald took the news stoically. For all his struggles with his work life at that moment, he felt like his home was secure and he could afford to take a few risks in the pursuit of appearing normal. While the revelation that their father was finally relaxing his rules a little might have brought relief to the rest of the family, none of them was foolish enough to mention that one of the other older children was dating. They were hopeful, but they weren't ready to abandon the safety of lies just yet.

This time, Ronald showed no hesitation before diving back into the job hunt. While he was growing more desperate each time he had to go looking for work again, he was also becoming pickier. This time, he scouted out his potential employers as though he were planning a mission in enemy territory. He selected a business where he would be working with fellow veterans and would not be answering to any women. His new position as a convenience store clerk did not pay nearly as well as his previous roles, the hours were much less consistent, and instead of dealing with only the odd customer over the telephone he was now on the front lines against the general public every single day.

He was miserable in the job, he absolutely loathed the work, he loathed customer service, and he considered the paltry amount of pay that he received for his suffering to be a grievous insult. While Ronald had looked on the people around him at his previous jobs as his inferiors due to their lack of discipline and service to the country he loved, he had some respect for his co-workers at the convenience store, one of whom had served as a marine in the Vietnam War. He had so much respect for the man, Bill Mason, that he didn't even bother to paste on a mask of false civility, coming as close to being honest with Bill as he had ever been with anyone in his life. Bill considered Ronald to be a gruff, angry man, but he wasn't any different from most of the veterans that he had met through the years. He was actually quietly impressed with Ronald sometimes, particularly when he helped out during a charity drive to collect Christmas presents for needy children in the area.

*

The rumours had reached Ronald through his working days—a stray comment from some housewife here or a wink and a nod from some chubby football coach there, all adding fuel to the flames of suspicion. He wouldn't confront her though. Not yet. He couldn't go to her half-cocked with hints and whispers. He needed proof before he could toss that treacherous bitch to the curb. He had given her the best years of his life, and this was how she repaid him? He had done everything for her. Provided everything for her. And now, when things got difficult, she was off fucking some other man? Ronald had stood for a lot in his time, disrespect and snide comments, conspiracies and spite. But adultery was a step too far. The ultimate disrespect. He was going to destroy her for this. Not just hurt her, not just kill her, he was going to burn her down and salt the earth. Just as soon as he could prove that she had strayed from his side. It was hardly the first time that the bitch had stabbed him in the back. He had been too soft with her then, accepting her lies and forgiving everything without a second thought. Well, he wasn't going to be fooled again. All of the tricksters and jezebels and liars were going to get their comeuppance, and that bitch was going to get hers first. He was going to fix her real good. He wouldn't even need his hands. Just the power of his words would be enough to tear her down and make her obedient again.

Bill passed him by in the aisle as he brushed out the store. Bill was a good man. He didn't even comment on the cans still clenched tight in Ronald's hands. He didn't ask what was wrong or try to force conversation with people that didn't want it. Ronald placed the cans down carefully on the shelf and went back to restocking. His shift would be over soon, and he needed to get things ship-shape before he drove home or he knew that it would bug him all night.

In the end, he left a half hour late, not that he would get paid for the extra time, of course. No point in paying a fair wage to a war hero. No point in paying people what they are worth. You could slump in through the door a minute before your timecard asked you to and disappear without even saying goodbye and nobody seemed to care. You got paid the same if you were good, bad, or indifferent. God help you if you took pride in your work and cared about things being done right, because there was no way that anybody else was going to give a damn.

He gave Bill a salute as he locked up and then clambered into his car. The radio crackled to life and a preacher started his ranting and raving. Damning all the sinners. It suited his mood perfectly. They were all sinners. Every one of them was damned. He was the last righteous man in all of Arkansas. A modern day Job surrounded on all sides by betrayers and tormenters. It was a wonder that he could tolerate even a moment longer. It wasn't like he hadn't told them. It wasn't like he hadn't showed them how everything needed to be done. Still they defied him. He was just trying to make everything right and they went against him for no better reason than being too damned lazy to learn. Well, that bitch would learn now. Oh yes, she would learn. He had done some bad things in his days. He was penitent, but not perfect. But adultery? He would never stoop so low. A car overtook him as he came out of town, its headlights flashing in his rear-view mirror as he growled. For a moment he caught a glimpse of Kathy's pretty green eyes in the light and he felt a tug in his guts.

That didn't count. That wasn't his fault. He had been led astray by that temptress. Swishing around in her short skirts. Fluttering those eyelashes every time he passed her by and then acting disgusted when he smiled back at her. It was a trap, a setup. She was trying to lead him astray from his one true love with that body of hers. She was a bitch, too. All of them were good for nothing except that one thing that the Lord put them on this earth to do. It wasn't like anything had even happened. Just because you are tempted doesn't mean you sinned. Besides, even if the bitch did know about Kathy, which she most certainly did not, it wouldn't justify stabbing him in the back like this. He was a good man, he took good care of his family, he deserved a woman who he could trust. Just one woman in all his life who wouldn't try to worm her way out of his arms while he was sleeping. One woman who wouldn't abandon him. Just one.

The drive back to Mockingbird Hill seemed to fly by that night, or maybe what happened afterwards just burned all the other memories away. When Ronald came up the drive in the waning twilight, he could see the gate sitting open ahead of him. That set him off grumbling before he even had time to ponder it. The kids knew better than to let the dog run loose. By the time he had made it over the top of the hill, he could see the other car parked in his yard, and it was all that he could do to keep from screaming. Someone was on his property. Someone was in his house. With his kids. With his girls. Without his permission. He slammed his foot on the brake. He smashed the palms of his hands against the wheel. His head spun as he tried to make sense of it. Police would have come in a marked car, probably. Military police, if they had ever gotten involved, would have been even more obvious. Could be a social worker. Those scum latched onto families like ticks on a dog's belly. The car looked too new, though. Social workers didn't have two pennies to rub together. Ronald gathered up all of his rage and bile, everything that had boiled up when he saw some stranger's car parked in his driveway, and he pushed it back down. He swallowed it all and put on his mask of civility in case it was just some damned fool who got lost on their way out into the middle of nowhere.

When he stepped in through the sliding windows of the living room, he realised rapidly that even if he didn't know who the visitor was, the rest of the family knew the boy damned well. There was tension hanging in the air like they were all about ten minutes away from the start of a bar brawl, and the second that he stepped inside, all eyes were on him. That wasn't so unusual. The kids knew to watch their father for guidance, and Becky was a good and attentive wife when she wasn't too busy with her head in the clouds. Becky had squirrelled the kids away in their rooms, which was unusual, but Sheila was missing, too. This boy must have been about her age. He was a local kid, the owner of the car outside. He probably knew her from school. So why wasn't she here? More importantly, what was this little shit doing sitting in the middle of his house as if he owned the place.

The boy got up from his seat, from Ronald's seat, that he bought and paid for, and lumbered over with a hand held out, like the damned dog begging for food. Ronald stared at it for a long moment, and he could see Becky shaking her head slowly from the periphery of his vision. He forced a smile and shook the boy's hand with a soft groan. He hissed out, 'Pleasure to meet you son.'

The boy smiled back, gregarious and bright without a care in the world. He gripped Ronald's hand as tight as he dared and squeezed until the older man could feel his bones grinding together.

'It is good to meet you, sir. My name is Dennis McNulty, and I wonder if I could trouble you and your wife for a few minutes to discuss some important matters.'

Ronald had to swallow back a sneer, as if this child would know important if it bit him on the ass. Dennis wandered back over and settled into that seat as if he belonged, even giving Becky a wink as he passed. Cocky little shit. Ronald went to the fridge to fetch himself a beer before perching himself at the far end of the sofa. He knew that he was scowling at the boy, but if this Dennis insisted on invading good people's homes uninvited then he deserved more than a dirty look or two. Eventually Ronald growled, 'What do you want boy?'

Dennis' smile never wavered. 'Right to the point. I like that. Well, Mr. Simmons, I have intentions to ask your daughter to marry me, already sort of did if the truth be told, but I wanted to speak to you about a few things before that went any further.'

Ronald's frown deepened as the whispers and rumours connected with the reality sitting in front of him. The bitch. It was true. He murmured, 'Sheila...'

For a moment it must have looked like he was going to cry at this irrefutable evidence that his love was straying from his side, but he swallowed that down, too, and tried to overwhelm the boy with bluster. 'Son, I love my daughter dearly, and I'm sure that she has been whispering all sorts of sweet nothings in your ears, but I don't think that you want to spend the rest of your life raising some other man's bastard, do you?'

Dennis' smile twitched a little. 'With all due respect sir, I love your daughter and I have spent some time with little Sylvia, too. I would be happy to call that little girl my daughter and raise her as my own.'

Ronald bit back a growl, 'Ain't you a little bit too young to be making big decisions like this? A child is a big responsibility. It ain't like a pet dog.'

Dennis carefully met his gaze. 'I would take my responsibilities very seriously, sir. I would take good care of your daughter and I would never abuse the trust that Sheila has put in me.'

Ronald narrowed his eyes. 'I'm not sure what you are getting at here, son. So let me cut to the chase. There ain't no way that I am letting you walk out of here with my daughter and that baby. Not tonight. Not ever.'

Becky made a little-strangled noise, but Ronald silenced her with a glance and a tut. Dennis smiled again. 'Sheila is already gone. Her and Sylvia were gone before you even arrived. They are in my apartment right now, getting themselves settled in. If it was up to her we would have just up and left without ever saying a word to you, but I believe in doing things right. I believe in talking straight with people, and I hope that they will do the same with me.'

Ronald was out of his chair before he even knew it and had crossed half of the floor before the next words out of Dennis' mouth stopped him dead in his tracks.

'Sheila told me all about you Mr. Simmons. She told me all about who her baby's daddy is. Like I said, I like honesty.'

Ronald slid to a halt, fists clenched at his sides and chest heaving. The boy stood up and closed the distance. He stared Ronald down every step of the way. His voice was only a little above a whisper when he finally said, 'She told me exactly what you did to her, sir. I know everything. That is why I wanted to speak to you tonight instead of just vanishing like a coward. So that you would know what I know and so that I could tell you this...' They were nose to nose. Ronald was shaking with barely restrained fury. Dennis finished. 'If you ever come near her or Sylvia again, if you lay a finger on either one of them, from now until the end of your miserable life. I will kill you. So help me god. I will kill you, sir.'

Then Dennis nodded politely to Becky and left without another word.

Over the days following Sheila's departure, when everyone expected that Ronald was going to explode, he instead fell completely silent. For a few weeks he went through his routine as usual, but when he got home, instead of assuming his place in the centre of the household to bark out orders, he collected a few bottles of beer from the fridge and withdrew to a darkened bedroom for the rest of the evening. He did not speak to anyone that he did not have to speak to, and he did not demand anything from his family. Out of habit, they maintained their usual routines, but all sense of urgency was gone. It seemed that his control over the family was finally broken. Along with him.

*

Without their father dominating every moment of their lives, the children began to experience normal lives for the first time. Their friendships were allowed to continue outside of school hours, and they were allowed to develop interests beyond serving their father's every demand. The changes were not limited to the children. Becky finally began to pull together the courage to leave her husband. Gene junior had re-established communication with his mother as soon as possible after fleeing, setting up a secret post box for her in town so that she could communicate without Ronald interfering with her mail. In her letters, Becky talked at great length about her fears and desires regarding starting a new life. Fear still dominated her, but it was a fear of the unknown, a fear of the uncertain circumstances that life away from Ronald would force her into. The fear of Ronald himself seemed to have faded as she saw him as the sad, bitter old man that he had become.

In the letters, she spoke at length about her previous attempts at leaving and the reasons that she believed that they had failed, placing the blame squarely on the fact that each attempt had been undertaken on the spur of the moment without any sort of planning. She did not want to have to rely on the kindness of her children for support as she tried to find her footing, and she had no idea what she would do with life outside of marriage. But she was finally finding the courage to take the final step and try. All that she wanted before fleeing the family forever was one last Christmas together. In her final letter, she wrote to her second son Billy:

> Dear Bill, Renata and Trae,
>
> Loretta, may be staying in town Friday night, so I'll have her mail this. I've been thinking of all you said Bill and I know you are right, I don't want to live the rest of my live with Dad, but I'm still trying to figure out how to start, what if I couldn't find a job for some time. You have to remember I've never had a job since I've been married, or before that either. I know I have to start somewhere. It would all be so much easier if it was just me, but I have three kids also by then. So if you want to do any checking by telephone go ahead and check and we can talk about it when you come. I've decided if I borrow from Mom, that I would have her send it to you. I'm still all very confused but like I said I do know I don't want to stay with Dad, but don't want him getting more than he deserves. Yet sometimes I feel God is telling me to be more patient. Right now, I'll just say do some checking and then it will help make my decision. I would like for Loretta to move with you after she turns 18. She wants to go to college, and

she can get a job too. I don't think San Antonio is the place for her.

Little Gene and Wilma are back together, but they want to try it out and try to come get Barbara. I'm sure enjoying Barbara, she is a sweet lovable, polite little girl. She is a good girl and we all love her and enjoy her so much. She always has us laughing.

I'm so proud of Trae. The last time you came, Dad wanted to know how come you didn't stay long enough to see him too.

Now that L. Gene and Wilma are back together I wish they could move from San Antonio. Barbara needs both her parents. They both been through so much I hope it works out. I love them both. Wilma wrote me a letter telling me she loves L. Gene very much, and she must, she went back to him, and I'm sure she has been hurt deeply. I want to see all my children happy.

I've remembered a lot what you said Bill, I am a prisoner here and the kids too. I know when I get out, I might need help, Dad has had me like a prisoner, that the freedom might be hard for me to take, yet I know it would be great, having my children visit me anytime, having a telephone, going shopping if I want, going to church. Every time I think of freedom I want out as soon as possible. I don't want to put any burden on my children, and I think its best while or before I get out too old. I want out, but it's the beginning, once I get a job and place than I can handle it with the mental support of my children I can do it. It was hard to talk in front of L. Gene. He had been having it so hard, and his problems were deeply in my mind. I felt sorry for him. I was so afraid what he might go back and do. You are lucky Bill, you have a very good wife, she had led you the right way, and that is toward God. She is very pretty, too. I've always thanked God for sending you a good wife, I'm thankful for Dennis too.

Give my darling Trae a lot of hugs and kisses for me. I love you all very much. Barbara gets bored if I take too long to write, so I hope I made sense in this letter. Hope Loretta can mail this Fri. or Sat., on her way home.

Love you very much.

Mom.

After a few weeks, Ronald quit his job at the convenience store, citing the low wages, long hours, and lack of respect as his reasons. But even the other staff recognised that he was not his usual self. For him to quit in a temper tantrum would have been entirely in character, but instead he just faded away in every aspect of his life. From the outside, it appeared as if he had given up entirely on everything. Everything in his life that he had once been passionate about and everyone who he had ever cared about in his own twisted way were forgotten in the light of this latest imagined betrayal. With no job to distract him, Ronald stayed in his room day and night drinking until the money began to run out. Any hope of regaining control seemed to be slipping through his fingers. When Becky brought up the subject of Christmas, he acquiesced almost without complaint. She placed an order with the Walmart in Russellville for gifts for the children using almost the last of the savings, which Ronald parted with without complaint. They bought and decorated a tree together, and Becky made some calls to bring all of her babies back under one roof for one last Christmas celebration together. Even Sheila was convinced to come back with the added security of her protective husband Dennis by her side. The stage was set for a heartwarming reunion of all of the people that Ronald's evil behaviour over the years had driven apart.

Alone in his dark room, Ronald had meticulously laid a very different set of plans.

Part 3: Open Warfare

Ronald drew in a breath of the stale, sickly sweet air and let his sticky eyes open onto the total darkness of his room. Out of possessive habit, he let his hand fall on the empty dip in the mattress beside him. It was cold, but even the dampness of her sweat had dried out under the constant assault of the storage heaters. If it weren't for that dip, you would never have known that she had been there at all. Becky had moved in with the kids a few weeks back, in that snide and casual way that women stab you in the back. She hadn't even said a word to him, just set up a little cot in their room and started locking the door at night. One of them had a fever one night, that was her excuse to start with, then it turned into habit and god knows, Becky was a creature of habit. Even after a lifetime together, Ronald hadn't been able to break her of some of them. She still wiped the dishes wrong and left them all smeared. Such a simple thing to understand; something half-cleaned is still dirty. But she just wouldn't wrap her head around it. She still couldn't be convinced to pick up after her spoiled self. He could see her bits and pieces littering the dresser even now. She wouldn't put things back where they belonged no matter how many times he showed her exactly how he wanted it done. She couldn't be that stupid, so he had to come up with his own excuses for her, bad habits or bad breeding.

It was going to be a relief not to make excuses for her anymore. It was going to ease Ronald's mind considerably not having to manufacture a daily list of reasons that his wife wasn't a disobedient, backstabbing traitor to the family. Ronald didn't like lying. Not from other people and certainly not from himself. He could lie when he needed to, when it was required for the mission or to protect his property, but it always left the world feeling jagged-edged and fuzzy. He had to hold that lie in his head all day long every day until everyone forgot about it, and every moment that he did was like torture. The world was the way that the world was. Confusing matters just made Ronald feel even less in control of it than he already did. Lying was just another way to oil his grip on things, and it made him queasy to think of the number of times that he had lied for his precious little wife. Lied to other people in talking about how good she was and lied to himself in making excuses for the horrible truth that she just didn't give a good goddamn about him and the family.

Ronald stretched out on the stale sheets, then an insistent pressure from his gut forced him to get up. Back in the old days, he would have been up like a shot, scrubbed and shaved and dressed before the sun was even peeking over the horizon, but now things were different. He was slowing down as the ache in his bones started to make getting up a chore. Even without the promise of pain, he was finding it hard to think of a reason that getting out of bed was worthwhile. His bladder gave another twinge, just to remind him. He swung his legs over the side of the bed and nearly slipped on the beer bottles lying scattered all around. Fury sparked instantly. Why the hell hadn't Becky cleaned this mess up? Then just as quickly, his iron control clamped down on that rage. She hadn't cleaned it up because she wasn't welcome in this room anymore. He wouldn't want a traitor in his bed. He picked his way carefully past the bottles and overflowing ashtrays and unlocked the door as gently as he could, bracing himself for the impending headache. When he pulled the door open, the pain didn't come. The hateful light of day wasn't streaming in through the patio doors to blind him and set his hangover screaming. Outside it was still blessedly dark.

A crooked smile appeared deep inside the thicket of Ronald's wild beard as he stepped out into the yard. This far from city lights, he could look up and see all the stars in the sky, every one of them locked in position in relation to one another, every one of them drifting around the sky in a perfectly predictable rotation. He drew in a deep breath of the freezing air and let it out in a huff of steam. Even if he had forgotten what day it was, some part of him remembered what it was like to wake up ready for a mission. Some part of him beyond his rational mind must have known that he needed this today, so he said a quiet prayer of thanks as he wandered over to the outhouse, carefully weaving around the new cesspit that the kids had been set to digging last month before the ground froze up. He had never had trouble sleeping the night before a new mission. He had always been able to trust in his body to haul him awake in plenty of time. It was nice to know that no matter how much some things changed, he could still rely on one person in this world to look out for him.

Despite the cold stabbing further up his legs, he still let the dog out of his house and tossed a handful of feed to the still drowsy chickens in the snake pit before heading back inside to get dressed. The dog was the only one who he never felt any anger towards. In their own way, dogs were perfectly predictable. Once you had put the time into training them, you could rely on them to go on doing as they were told for the rest of their lives. You didn't have to worry about them snapping at your fingers when you tried to feed and shelter them. You didn't have to worry about them tearing your throat out while you were sleeping. You didn't have to worry about them sneaking around making plans with other dogs to run away. If they did any of that, then man would have done away with the whole species, stopped inviting them into their homes.

If only they had been so wise about women.

Ronald squatted awkwardly, hips complaining all the while, to give the dog a pat on the head as it passed. Then he went off to prepare for today's mission. The dog knew better than to bark. It had learned how vital silence was. It bounded around the yard joyfully in the starlight until Ronald sent it back to its doghouse with a snap of his fingers, flipped the latch, and then drove off into town before the rest of the family had even begun to stir.

Ronald could feel the tension building in his gut as he drove. Not the anxiety that plagued lesser men, but that horrible churning of adrenaline and excitement that only a soldier truly knows. The rich and intoxicating brew that lets you move, think, and kill while bullets fly all around you. With nothing to distract him, he turned inwards and drove in silence amidst the storm of his thoughts. In Russellville, he went through the motions in the Walmart, handing over the money that was meant to last them until he could find a new job in exchange for a shiny new .22 calibre pistol and a box of ammunition. The drive home flashed by just as quickly, and all too suddenly he was driving up the red clay track to Mockingbird Hill once more. Running through his plan, backwards and forwards until he was certain that every moment of the timing was right. He parked the car to one side so that his visitors would have plenty of room, then he stalked slowly across to the sliding doors and checked inside for anything resembling a surprise. Becky remained predictable in her mediocrity. She was huddled at the kitchen table staring off into space. The kids were off to school by now, and while that particular clock was ticking, it was ticking very slowly. He had all day to do his work and very little work to do. He backed away carefully and went to check on the yard.

The dog was still stowed away safely, and the tarpaulin-covered cesspit hadn't been disturbed by the damned kids fooling around. His tools were all bundled up in oilcloth by the latest junker that he had been stripping for scrap and spare parts. Everything of value had been peeled off of the old car and sold off to fund this Christmas foolishness that Becky insisted on indulging in. The sweat of his brow and the ache of his muscles had earned that money, and every time he spent a penny of it, he knew she was sitting there in that kitchen disapproving. How was it selfish for a man to spend his own money? How was it selfish for a man to expect his own wife to be obedient? How was it selfish to not want your children growing up into spoiled little brats like the hippie spawn that he saw milling around in town, knocking over cans of soup and giggling when he had to clear them away? The whole world might be sighing and tutting at Ronald, but he knew that he was in the right. He knew that in time they would all come to realise it, too. He lifted the crowbar out of the pack and hefted its rusted weight in his hands. He could feel his joints creaking, but he still had all of his strength. He wouldn't wither like some old men did. He was still a man of action. He still had the time to do what he needed to do before he was too old to do it. He considered the crowbar, then he considered the pistol tucked into his belt. He still had plenty of time.

He made a point of making a noise as he entered the house this time, keeping the crowbar hanging behind his leg, out of sight, just in case Becky was suddenly overcome with the urge to leap up and greet him. He was just stalking through to his room when he saw little Barbara's door swing open. Gene Junior stepped out backwards, still keeping his eye on the little girl to make sure she stayed settled in her nap. He jumped when he spotted his father. He was ruining it. He wasn't supposed to be here yet. He was ruining it. Ronald must have walked right past his car without even thinking about it twice. That worthless son of a bitch. That boy was the worst thing that ever slithered out of his worthless mother. Ronald still had his suspicions about who had turned him in back in New Mexico. He had never pegged Becky as having the guts, even if she was the one who caught hell for it at the time. Little Gene was the prime suspect after her. He had always been a source of trouble. His mother had been useless but at least obedient before that brat came along. Ronald wished that the boy had never been born. That boy was the biggest mistake he had ever made in his entire life. His grip on the crowbar tightened. Gene opened his mouth to spit out some new poisonous lie, but he only got as far as, 'Dad?' before Ronald swung.

It hit the boy right in the centre of his forehead. Gene staggered, cross-eyed as if he were trying to see where the crowbar had hit him. Ronald slammed it down again and again. The boy fell to his knees against one of the chairs, mouth hanging open like some kind of moron, eyes out of focus. Ronald sneered at the boy's weakness as the runt gasped and drooled. He brought the crowbar down on Gene's face once more, popping his nose with a gristly splatter and knocking the boy out cold. Gene hefted the crowbar and gave the boy one last whack across the skull for good measure, just to be sure. It jarred right up the length of his arm.

His own head was spinning. The adrenaline rush that would have carried him through the whole mission smoothly was all but spent, and he was gasping for breath after just one target was down. He tried to realign his plans and in a blissful moment realised that this made everything so much easier. Gene Junior was the random element in all of this. He could have shown up at just the wrong moment and made things much more difficult. It might have startled him, but there was no way that this could have gone better. Ronald looked down at his son, leaking blood from his nose and his ears onto the flea-market rug that covered half the room, and gave him the first smile that the boy had earned since he was a day old. He stomped firmly on the boy's midsection to make certain that he wasn't going to pop up unexpectedly again. Air was driven out of Gene's body in a bubbling red stream, and he made a noise that might have been a groan but that Ronald hoped was a death rattle. That boy had this coming to him since a long time ago, but he had always been up front about his hatred of his father, and Ronald could respect him for that.

The noise had disturbed Becky from her spot in the kitchen. If Ronald had known that committing bloody murder in the room next door was all it took to get Becky moving, he would have started doing it years ago. It wasn't like they had a shortage of kids to beat to death. He repositioned himself by the door to the kitchen, briskly striding around the carnage that he had wrought without a glance back. This was better than he could have dreamed. At the end of the day, Gene was the first man she had betrayed him for. The first one who had made her disregard her husband's wishes. It was kind of poetic that she would see that boy broken, pathetic, and drooling on the floor before death came to her. She let out a gasp when she stepped into the room, and then she froze. Just like Ronald had always known that she would. She was weak. From the top of her hair to the tips of her toes. Ronald's first blow could have landed anywhere he chose. She was so lost in her own world of panic he could have walked right up to her face and started swinging away, but that wasn't the plan.

He hit her across the shoulders and she tumbled to the ground in a heap. She was the first to betray him. The rest had just been following her lead. They were all traitors, but she was the one who had led them astray. She was the one who they trusted and the one who had betrayed all of them, too, when she turned them against him. He rained blows down on her. Somehow she found her voice after all these years of silence, screeching each time the crowbar bounced off of her back. He felt a rib or two give way, but it wasn't enough. She had to hurt like he hurt. She had to feel what he felt. She had to know what it was like to be torn apart by the one person who you were meant to be able to trust the most. He stopped his flurry of blows for a long moment to draw a breath, then he flipped the crowbar over in his hand so that the jagged teeth were now raised up. He looked down at the expanse of her floral print dress like an artist looks at a canvas, then he started painting red flowers of his own. He watched them blossom as the bitch wailed and wailed. The noises stopped being human after the first dozen hunks of meat were torn loose from her. It turned into a guttural grunting noise like some hulking beast trying to haul itself out of the sea. It was a mercy killing. By the time that he stopped swinging, there could be no denying that it was a mercy killing.

He drew out the pistol and put a round in the back of her head, just to be sure. He strolled across the room and gave the boy the same treatment, right in the dark bruise between his eyes. The room smelled sharp as the taste of a penny. He would have to deal with that, too. Couldn't have any surprises getting spoiled. Startled awake by the gunshots, little Barbara began to cry.

Ronald glanced at his watch as if his cuffs weren't flecked with his wife's blood. Barely five minutes had passed since he first opened the door. He chuckled to himself and decided to take a break. This was harder work than he would have thought, and he hadn't even gotten to the heavy lifting yet. He fetched a beer out of the fridge and settled himself by the kitchen table, tapping out one of Becky's cigarettes and lighting it with practiced ease. He let the familiar flavours and the familiar motions soothe him as he planned out his next moves. This had been almost startlingly easy. He couldn't understand why more people didn't do it. Sure, he might be a little sore in the morning, but what did a few pulled muscles matter compared to peace of mind. He drew on the beer again and forced himself to smile. He was hurting, but he was putting it right. One body at a time, he was putting it right. The next steps were the most laborious—disposing of bodies and... he stopped. He couldn't concentrate with that ceaseless caterwauling going on. Why wasn't Becky shutting that damned child up?

He let out a snort as he realised. Then he set his beer down with a clunk. There was no rest for the righteous. He walked through to little Barb's room with the pistol held behind his back.

There was no point in scaring the girl. It wouldn't make his job any easier, and besides, it wasn't like she had much of a chance to screw things up yet. When she looked up at him with her big tearful eyes, he tucked the pistol away out of sight. He bent down low and wrapped his arms around her, and she didn't know what to do because he had never given her more than a barked order and a glance before. The tears stopped immediately. His hands slipped up her skinny little body to the back of her neck. Then they slipped around it. Then he started to squeeze. He closed his eyes but he could still feel her. He could still feel the warm meat of her throat caught between his worn hands and the desperate fluttering of her heartbeat where his fingertips bit into her flesh. He could feel her bones grinding in his grip. It was less like choking a person and more like crushing a baby bird. If she struggled, it was so weakly that he did not notice, and if she cried he could not hear her over the rush of blood in his ears. He let her drop back onto her bed after he was done. This room didn't smell of blood, at least. Only the acrid stink of urine hung in the air over Little Barb's body, as if she had pissed the bed in her sleep again one last time instead of having it wrung out of her like a dirty towel.

 Ronald ambled back through to the living room and flicked on the TV. He still had work to do, and he had no plans of slacking off, but the background noise would help calm the screaming still rattling around in his skull. It would drown out the little gasps and the echoes of the gunshots that were still bouncing around in his ears. He finished his beer and then set to work dragging the corpses outside. He lifted the cinderblock off one corner of the cesspit and folded the tarpaulin away. Running through each step just as he had imagined it. With the tarp pinned back, he tossed the ruin of Becky and the body of Gene Junior into the hole then kicked them across to the far side to make more room. He snatched up the crowbar and threw that in with them too, just to be sure not to forget it later. Barbara's sodden clothes presented a whole other problem to navigate.

Just the thought of handling a piss-soaked corpse made Ronald's stomach turn. He fetched a black refuse sack from in the kitchen and stuffed her in as quickly as he could, touching her as little as he could manage. She was still as warm as a living girl. Out at the pit, he lowered the sack that held Barbara down beside her mother with more gentleness than he had ever intended.

Ronald swiped at his eyes with his cuff. This was the mission. This was the only option that they had left him. Getting soft wouldn't change the facts. It would just make him a weakling and a coward on top of everything else. He knew that he was alone up here on Mockingbird Hill. He knew that nobody could see what he did here, but even so, he wouldn't let any son of a bitch see him cry, even if it was the big man up in the sky. He fetched out a can of kerosene from beside the generator and sprinkled it over his wife and kids. The charnel house stink in the pit subsided as the vapours of the kerosene overpowered it. He had some spare barbed wire to drag over the pit once it was full, to keep wild animals from gnawing at them or hauling them out into the open. But he wasn't going to go to the trouble of fetching his thick gloves until he was done for the day.

Back in the house, Ronald made a half-hearted attempt to mop the blood away and left the doors standing open so that the smell would air out. He had to get things under control before the kids got back from school. He went back to running through the plan in his mind, and as he slipped back into that rational mode of thinking, his movements became more controlled. He mopped down the linoleum floor of the mobile home with all the precision he had once used on the decks of a ship. He stripped Little Barb's bed, tossing the contents into another refuse sack that he added to the septic pit before covering it over and replacing the cinderblock that hides his morning's work. He threw one of Becky's good towels on the mattress to soak up the last of the piss and then went back to fetch his last beer from the fridge. He settled himself down in front of the television with his arm propped up beside him so that the watch was aimed right at his face. He laid the pistol beside his other hand, just in case any more surprises presented themselves and interfered with his perfectly scripted plan.

The hours turned by slowly. The television had never held his interest. It was just something to stare at while he waited for his next task. Nothing on the screen made it further than his eyes. Inside, he was still turning his plan over in his mind endlessly. Quashing any treacherous voice of resistance or reluctance that he might have found lurking in his head. When the time came, he tucked the gun back into his belt, covered it with his jacket and went down to meet his kids as they came off the school bus.

The four Simmons kids didn't know how to handle their father meeting them from the bus at the bottom of their driveway. It was the first time he had ever taken an interest beyond the mandatory, and most days they would take their time strolling up the slope just to have more time free of him. Was this his latest attempt to control their lives? Just popping up at random points during the day when they didn't have to deal with him? Their natural suspicion must have shown on their faces because he sniggered and said, 'Christmas is coming. Your mom likes surprises. You work it out.'

He congratulated himself on the delivery of that simple sentence because it set the four of them whispering amongst themselves, completely distracted from anything that he might be doing. Better yet, it wasn't even a lie. Just a statement of some random facts. He didn't have to hold it in his mind. He didn't have to trick the world into believing it. He just had to keep on walking. The actual lie would come up at the house, but there he would only have to sustain it for a brief moment. They walked past the grave of their mother, brother and sister without noticing a thing out of place. The red clay of the earth covered up any gory stains nicely.

He led them through to their rooms and finally let the lie tumble out as smoothly as he could: 'There's a special surprise for each of you, but your mom wants to see each of you enjoy yours, so you're to come through one at a time when I come to fetch you.'

All four of their faces lit up as he told them. It was the happiest that he could ever remember seeing them, but then again, he didn't usually bother to look at their faces. Their height and hair were enough to tell them apart, and if he sometimes yelled the wrong name it didn't do the other one any harm to have a scare to keep them in line. He took Loretta through first, leading her through the living room where the faint metallic smell of blood still lingered to his adrenalin heightened senses. Out through the sliding doors and around to the water barrel at the rear side of the building. He turned to look at her. Sweet Loretta was as old as Sheila had been when she first turned on him. She had her sister's eyes, her heart shaped face. His love for Loretta had never been as intense or as turbulent as his feelings towards Sheila, and he had never laid a hand on her in the way that people about town might have sneered at and called wrong, even if she did belong to him. The hair was wrong, the height was wrong, and even a casual glance at her all bundled up in her heavy jacket told him that the body was all wrong, but she was still just close enough to being Sheila that it made things simple.

Ronald grabbed a handful of her hair and shoved her face through the ice on the top of the water barrel. She bucked and tried to get a grip on the barrel's edge to pull herself out, but that first gasp of shock when the cold water hit her face had already done half the work of drowning her. She was his child as much as that bitch Becky's, so she had some fight in her. When she discovered that she couldn't push back against his weight holding her down she reached up and tried to claw at his hands. Her nails were kept clipped short like all his girls.—he wouldn't put up with any of the sluttish nonsense of growing them long and painting them.—so they skittered across the leathery skin of his hands leaving nothing more than a trace of dead skin lifted up. In reply, he jammed her neck down against the rim of the barrel and put his full weight on her. In his mind, he recited his plan over and over. This was the easy part. The quiet part. The part with no risk. He knew that they had betrayed him. He knew that they were defying him at every turn. This was what they deserved. He felt a dull clunk as the full weight of his body and the unbending edge of the metal crushed together through the soft tissue of her neck. Her struggles stopped instantly. Ronald hauled her to the septic pit and tossed her in. There was no blood and no screaming this way. It made everything so much easier. He went to fetch Eddy next.

One by one he went through the motions. Eddy didn't struggle like Loretta. He seemed surprised for a moment, then just seemed to accept his fate. Marianne jammed her elbow back into her father's face once the water hit her skin, and she probably would have been able to fight her way free of a man who lacked the determination that completely filled Ronald. Little Becky was the last. She was too short to reach over the top of the water barrel, so he led her to the edge of the septic pit full of corpses, wrapped his fingers around her little throat and squeezed the life out of her until her face turned purple and her eyes rolled up into her head. If she fought him he couldn't remember, but he suspected that she died helpless and hopeless just like her mother. Submitting when she knew that she was beaten. He didn't know if he could call that cowardice, and after this busy day, he didn't have the space left in his brain to think it through.

He poured some more kerosene over the corpses and then fetched out his good gloves and the barbed wire, cursing the vicious stuff each time he felt it prickling at him through his coat. He went as slowly as he could, laying it crisscrossed over the layer of bodies in the pit as though it was just another chore, but he was losing sunlight so quickly that he had to rush more than he would have liked. He rolled the tarp back over and dropped the cinderblock in place with a groan. It had been a long day and he was cursing himself for forgetting to pick up a six-pack while he was in town. At least he wouldn't have to worry about anyone pretending that they weren't scowling at him when he went to pick some up in the morning.

Ronald waited out the days until his next targets came into sight. He was a sharpshooter, and he knew just how the game was played. Unlike his military days, he had the comforts of home all around him, as much beer as he could carry, and most comforting of all, the exact time that each target was going to reach the spot where he was waiting. Becky had been planning Christmas for months. She had gone on and on and on about it until he was about ready to tear her head off, but instead, he had swallowed the fury down and forced himself to absorb the details as if it was a mission briefing. Becky might not have realised it at the time, but she was the enemy. She had been the enemy from the first moment that she had turned against him. Every word that she spoke was intercepted intelligence, even if it was difficult to consider a single word that she mumbled out to be anything resembling intelligent. She had been feeding him enemy positions, numbers, and supply lines since he first gave her a handful of cash for a Christmas tree. Ronald just wished that he had thought to buy the Vietcong a Christmas tree or two while he was over visiting them.

As much as the traitors who had slipped through his fingers might have loved their mother, they hadn't been willing to sacrifice their Christmas Day itself. Boxing Day had been portioned off to visit their own flesh and blood, while the scum that they were shacking up with were considered a priority on the holy day itself. If he hadn't loathed Becky so thoroughly by the end, he might have felt sorry for her, watching her wilt as every one of her children stabbed her in the back just the same way that they had turned on him the moment he showed a moment of weakness. Their arrivals were to be staggered through the day, ostensibly because of different travelling times, but really as a way to create a buffer. Billy, his wife Renata, and their runt Trae were due first, at around about midday. They were going to test the waters and make sure that their miserable old monster of a father wasn't going to cause any trouble before Sheila arrived with her little white knight an hour or so later, along with the baby she had stolen and the bastard she had birthed to the filthy little usurper who had stolen her from her loving family in turn. It would not stand. Ronald would not stand for it. Not for another moment. That was his girl. That was his baby. He made them both. He brought them both into the world. How dare that boy snatch her from his grasp. She belonged to him. Ronald brought his temper back under control as he watched the clock ticking around to midday. He only had to contain it for a little longer. All of the fury. All of the ways that he had been wronged. It was all going to be washed away. He was going to get them all and not a single tremor of anger would be left inside him. The static that had been shrieking between his ears since the moment his father died would fall silent. He knew this. He had absolute confidence that when these wrongs were righted, he would be able to live as other men lived, riding on the wave of chaos instead of being drowned beneath it.

The clock ticked around to midday, and he was out of his seat like a bullet out of a gun, stalking first to the door then the windows, looking out towards the driveway and then back to the patio doors again so he could look out and reassure himself that nobody and nothing had been troubling his septic pit. He had chased the dog away from it a couple of times over the last few days when it was let out of its pen, and he was going to let his .22 chase it off if it tried to snack on his dead babies again. They were all loathsome traitors who deserved nothing more than burial in a pit dug for an outhouse, but they were still his, and the dog had no right to them. He stumbled back and forth through the house, pacing and waiting and grumbling for a full five minutes before he heard tires coming up the driveway.

He grinned despite himself at the sound of gravel and wet clay being flung up against mudguards. He tried to force the smile down and then realised what a perfect disguise it would be.

With his beard all turned white he probably looked like a jolly old Santa Claus right now. He waited patiently by the door for as long as he could, listening as the engine was turned off, listening as they got out of the car, listening as they got their brat out of the back seat, then he pulled the door open and took a step back, grin still fixed in place. He flicked the safety off his pistol and drew in a steadying breath. Any second now.

Billy came up first, placing his wife and child behind him, safe from harm, like a real man should. It would have been enough, once upon a time, to make Ronald forget all the ways that this boy had tried to do him harm. It would have been enough to give him a spark of pride. As it was, all that it did was delay him in raising his arm just long enough for Billy to see the gun and let out a gasp before the first bullet took him right in the sternum. The bullet punched through his heart and then rattled around, bouncing off his ribs. Billy looked from the gun in his father's hands down to the dark wet patch on his shirt as though he couldn't put the pieces of the puzzle together. As if he didn't know what he had done. As if he didn't deserve a thousand times worse.

Renata was a brave girl. When she saw her husband hurt, she rushed forward to help him. She was a pretty thing, too. Lovely thick hair. It was a shame that the far side of it filled up so suddenly with fragments of skull and juicy pink brain matter as the bullet tore through her head. Ronald gently exhaled then tucked the still hot gun back into his trousers, letting the heat seep into his bones and ease his aches as he lumbered out into the cold. Their little boy Trae was out there, gaping at his parents' corpses and shaking. He smelled like he had pissed himself. What was it with these children and pissing themselves? Didn't they know how inconvenient it was? When Ronald came out of the house the kid lost all strength in his legs at the sight of him. Ronald would have laughed if it weren't so pathetic, to think that his blood had been diluted to that. He scooped Trae up and carried him to the water barrel. The ice was thinner this time, so there was no satisfying crunch as he threw the child in, but it was much sweeter to hold him by his ankles, completely submerged, than just push his head under. No matter how the boy writhed and wriggled there was nowhere for him to go. When he stopped squirming around, Ronald just let go and let the worthless little runt fold up on himself in the barrel, out of sight and out of mind.

There was still an hour to go before Sheila arrived. That was plenty of time to make his way back around to the front of the house and haul the bodies inside. Ronald lined the corpses up neatly in the middle of the room as if they were laid out for a funeral, tugged off their coats to cover their slack-jawed faces, and gave himself a pat on the back that it had only taken him half of the hour he had to do the job. He stood perfectly still for a few minutes, then carefully reloaded his gun. He double-checked the scene outside, to make sure it didn't look suspicious, and to make sure that there was plenty of room for her car to pull up, before strolling back inside.

He settled down with a fresh bottle of beer and stared down at the covered corpses as though they were the television set, without a single spark of recognition showing in his eyes or a single thought about what he was looking at firing off behind them. Christmas carols still played on the radio, but he couldn't even hear them. All of Ronald's plans had been leading to this moment, and the anticipation was almost overwhelming. The one who had ruined it all was coming here to face him. The monster who had destroyed him. Who had destroyed their family. The love of his life. He couldn't believe that even after all these years he still hadn't scrubbed her out of the place where she had burrowed into his heart.

He double-checked the gun. He finished the beer. He ran through the plan, over and over and over. There was so little of it left that it looped back almost as soon as it got started. This was the grand finale. This was the greatest enemy that he had ever faced in his life, the greatest betrayer. He closed his eyes and drew a steadying breath, just like they teach you in

Marksmanship 101. He drew it in, held it, and then let it ease out. He let the calm spread out through his body. He let it steady his hands.

He opened his eyes and listened carefully to the sound of the approaching car. In the corner of the room, the lights on the Christmas tree flickered on and off, dousing the shadows in a bath of colours that he stared into with the same mindless intensity as the bodies or the television. He breathed deeply and steadily as he heard a little girl shouting and laughing outside, overcome with exuberance at seeing her family again. It reminded him of his little Sheila at that age, so bright and perfect every moment of the day. He listened carefully for the sound of her voice. He wanted to hear her one last time before it was over, despite everything that she had done to him. He cursed himself for a fool, but he kept the gun hidden away just the same. The boy knocked on his door, too rough to have been any of the little girls out there, and with a quaver in his voice, Ronald called out, 'Come on in. We're all waiting for you.'

Dennis walked in first, holding Sylvia's hand. Holding Ronald's daughter's hand as if she belonged to any other man but him. It was the first time that he had seen his little girl in years. His lip quivered as he tried to hold back his tears. Then Sheila came into sight. She had cut her hair. She was dressed up like one of the women about town. He could have walked past her without realising it was his own daughter if it hadn't have been for her face. Those eyes and those lips still called to him. Even if they were smeared with garish red whore's war paint now. They crept into the room as though it were a bear's cave instead of a family home. The little boy Michael must have looked like his father, because Ronald couldn't see a trace of himself in that little face peeking around Sheila's skirts. Ronald gave Dennis as polite a smile as he could manage. 'Come on in. Let's have a talk.'

They crept in, getting closer and closer while still exuding fear. Even that brave boy Dennis, who had so proudly stood up to Ronald not so long ago, seemed to be quaking in his boots.

When they saw the bodies on the ground they froze in place. Ronald chuckled. 'What do you think boy? Do you still think you're going to kill me if I touch my own girl again? Do you think that you are anything to me except a waste of a bullet?'

He snapped off a shot and it burst through Dennis' chest, spraying blood up the wall behind him, sprinkling red to match the whore's lipstick across all of their Sunday finery. Sheila had known her father the longest and the best, so she didn't even try to run as he rose up from his seat to face her in all his fury. He levelled the gun at the swell of her chest and hissed, 'You have destroyed me. You have destroyed your mother, your brother, your sisters. You have destroyed all of us. You are a traitor and I will see you in hell.'

He squeezed the trigger. It only took one bullet to kill her, but it didn't feel like enough. She didn't feel dead enough yet. He unloaded the rest of the magazine into her corpse, each shot launching another gory spout up to stain the walls, the Christmas tree, and her bastard children.

He cast aside the pistol and snatched up that boy who looked nothing like him, that hideous depravity that his daughter had wrought on the world. He wrapped his shaking hands around that wrong thing and he ground his hands together as if it was the only way to keep the world from ending. He crushed that little boy's throat until he was certain that he would never breathe again, then he took a staggering step to toss the tiny corpse out into the mud. He spat after the boy and would have done worse if he didn't have other business to attend to.

The last victim of Sheila's treachery was crouched down beside the man who had stolen her, trying to shake him awake. It was intolerable. Even now, after he had won, after he had won so completely that there was no way for anyone to come back from it, this child was still acting as if the lie was true. As if this usurper had ever been her father. Ronald took her in his arms and she cried out, trying to get away. All the fight that had been missing from the bastard was here in the true heir to the

Simmons name. It was almost a shame to bring it all to an end. Still, it had to end. It all had to end and this was how. He put his hands almost gently around the girl's throat as she beat at him and screamed. He let her tear at him with her painted nails and shriek right up until the moment that she found that she couldn't make another sound. Her eyes went wide as he choked the life out of her. Staring right into his. Daring him to look away. She would have been a daughter who he could have been proud of. This all could have been avoided if it hadn't been for her mother ruining everything for everyone. She slapped at his hands weakly, as if she could sense his mind wandering. He met her stare and watched the life drain out of her. He kept on squeezing long after it all should have been over, as if letting go meant finally admitting that it was over.

Part 4: The Last Stand

He carried her by the neck to the other bodies and laid her down, stripping off her coat and covering her face. He dragged the boy who pretended at being her father over to lie him down beside her. Sheila should have been next, but he couldn't bring himself to lay her down there with the rest of the scum. He hefted her in his arms like he had when she was a little girl, cradling her tight against his chest as the heat left her body. He laid her carefully on the dining table and fetched out Becky's finest tablecloth to cover her up. It was the least that he could do for the love of his life. Blood began to soak through the thin cheap cloth almost immediately, but he didn't even look back. He still had the final motions of his mission to complete.

He collected some of the thick plastic wrapping that he used for parts from under one of the rusted hulks. He wrapped up the bastard brat sprawled on the mud, trying to touch him as little as possible, then he went to fetch the car keys from inside. He dumped him, unworthy as he was to lie among the Simmons dead, into the boot of his father's car and then drove it off to rest amongst the other junkers. He scooped the other pathetic worm from where he was still dangling limply in the water barrel before repeating the process with Billy's car. He went into the house to sprinkle some of the kerosene around and damp down the smell. Then it was over. The mission was accomplished. He staggered inside and changed into clean clothes before casting a glance over the living room. His eyes skimmed past the parts that he didn't want to see. He was done.

He had no idea what to do now. He had no plan to guide him. He stopped himself from losing control. He pulled himself back. He reminded himself that the time for that was all over now. He was the victor in this little war of his, so it was time to celebrate. He was going to a bar for the first time in as long as he could remember, he was going to drink whatever he wanted and he was going to worry about absolutely nothing. It was a quiet night in the bar, only the sad and the serious went out drinking a day after Christmas, even out here in the back end of nowhere. Ronald took his time and savoured the taste of real beer and the smoke in the air. Even the peanuts on the bar tasted better, even if they felt like styrofoam in his mouth.

He was free.

Nobody had a hold on him now. Nobody could go sneaking around telling filthy stories about what he did or didn't do. There would be no more Becky like a lead weight hanging around his neck, dragging him down into the dirt with her. There would be no more kids shrieking and screaming and running all around the house at all hours. His home would be a place of peace, a sanctuary from the outside world. All the evil in the world had died with the betrayer. He replayed the moment in his mind. The splatter of blood on the Christmas tree lights, tinting the room. The look on her face when she realised what she had brought down upon herself. She would not mistake his warnings again. Nobody would. When he had said that a reckoning was coming, he had most assuredly meant it.

He didn't know it, but Ronald's gruesome grin was making even the hearty drunks out on Boxing Day anxious. In the dim light of the bar, all that they could see was the bulging whites of his eyes and the glint of his teeth amidst the tangle of his beard.

He wheezed with laughter, replaying the memory over and over. The squeeze of the trigger. The pop of her chest as the bullet tore through her. Just like he had practiced. Centre of mass. Perfect shot. Every time. He savoured every detail of it. This would sustain him through the cold years that would come in a way that liquor and food never had.

The next morning, the itch was still there. Something that was still missing. Some vital part of his plan that had escaped his notice. His energy had returned and he rose with the dawn. He paced as usual, let the dog run around the yard and slowly realised what was missing. An ending. He was not so foolish to think that this slaughter would go unnoticed forever, nor was he cowardly enough to flee from whatever justice confronted him, so long as he remained in control of the situation. The only thing that still weighed on him, the only thing that he could not control throughout the whole thing, would be how the rest of them would respond, all of the other enemies who had aligned themselves against him through his years in Russellville. He couldn't stand the thought of them snickering and talking behind his back. He could not tolerate the idea of them still being in the world when he was gone, at all. He sat with the television on, drinking beer all day long as the new plan slotted together in his mind. Once all the pieces were there, there was only one logical way for them to fit together. He sat still and watched the television and drank his beer, three feet away from the rotting corpses of his family, and he did not get up and leave because his plan required him to wait. It was a Sunday after all.

He drove into Russellville first thing the next morning in Gene Junior's car, stopping by the Walmart to restock on ammo before heading straight to the offices of Peel, Eddy, and Gibbons Law Firm. He wore a straw cowboy hat as a feeble disguise, but there was no way that Kathy Kendrick did not recognise him before he pulled the trigger. Inside their offices, the lawyers and secretaries in the back heard her shouting and heard the gun firing off, but they did not move. Some of them believed that it was some children playing with a new noisy Christmas toy. But to others it seemed weird that someone firing a gun in a law office was not gunning for one of the lawyers. They kept their heads down until they were certain that Ronald was gone, by which time it was far too late for the poor girl who had become his final obsession. One of the lawyer's clients was waiting in the front room and saw it all unfold in front of her. After Simmons made his swift exit she started screaming, 'He shot her! He shot her!' over and over until a legal secretary emerged from the back to investigate. There was a bullet-hole in the wall above Kendrick's desk, and her body was found slumped on the ground. There was blood pouring out of a wound on the back of her head. Blood so bright and red that it surprised the onlookers. She was still alive when they found her. They said that she was still breathing despite the bullet having gone right through her head, although she had faded before an ambulance could arrive. Nobody knew who had shot her. Nobody knew why he had done it.

Whatever emotion Ronald had left seemed to have been spent, and now he was just going through the necessary motions. At his next stop, Ronald switched his hat for a baseball cap and came out with his gun at the ready in case warning had been called ahead. The Taylor Oil Company had no warning at all of what was about to descend upon them. Ronald started firing on sight, gunning down J. D. Chaffin, one of the truckers and a volunteer fireman with almost casual contempt, just because he walked into Simmons' line of sight at the wrong moment. The man died at the scene. Ronald set his sights on his actual target next. Russell 'Rusty' Taylor was the owner of both Taylor Oil and the Sinclair Mini-Mart where Ronald had found his final place of employment. Russell was hit twice and badly wounded before another worker arrived on the scene, wandering back through from the bathroom. Julie Money had just started as the bookkeeper for the oil company. She thought that all of the noise and theatrics were probably the latest in a series of good-natured pranks that the boys had been playing on her since she started.

She froze in place when she spotted Chaffin's body, and before she could unfreeze Simmons had his revolver pressed to her forehead. Thoughts of her two children danced through her head. She screamed, 'No!' and leapt for cover as he pulled the trigger. The bullet seared a line through her short blonde hair as she fell behind some crates. She had the good sense to play dead. Ronald fled the scene, laying down a flurry of covering fire that missed everyone present. Russell Taylor was saved by paramedics before the next call for help even came in.

Ronald Simmons went through his entire spree expecting armed resistance from the people of the town. He kept on expecting them to realise that they were at war with him, but all that they saw were the actions of a madman. If anyone in town had paid attention to the strange monster dwelling amongst them, then his next stop might have been predictable. But despite the town's tiny population and Ronald's unusual appearance, he had been so reclusive that nobody was able to make the connection before he arrived at the store where he had been working little more than a month before. He reloaded his pistol in the car as he drove, with a practiced ease born from hours on the firing range. He switched hats once more and strode gleefully into the Mini-Mart, ready to unleash hell on the last in the long list of places where he felt he had been belittled and insulted. He walked right up to the counter, looked his old co-worker Rebecca Woolery in the eye and the shot her right in the chest. The manager, David Salyer, heard the bang and came running from the back of the shop. He had only an instant before Simmons turned the gun on him, and he spent it throwing a chair at the man. It was enough to knock off the marksman's perfect aim. The bullet hit Salyer, knocking him to the ground, but the injury would not prove any more fatal than Woolery's. Both victims would survive, because an unexpected third party intervened before Simmons could deliver a killing blow.

Ronald was not the only one in the store who had seen combat. The store's other veteran, Bill Mason, had been stocking shelves just out of sight and responded to the threat with trained efficiency. He began pelting Ronald with full cans of soda, interrupting any attempt to aim and preventing him from delivering a coup de grace on either of the fallen Mini-Mart workers. Under attack for the first time since the beginning of his great mission, Ronald retreated to the car and sped off, flustered.

In the car, rage began to overpower Ronald once again. This was going to be the end of his life and they were even trying to spoil that. They were interfering in his plans. They were ruining everything. His final stop in town was Woodline Motor Freight. He had learned from his mistakes, stepping out of the car and walking calmly through the offices, doing his best to ignore the other workers who had crossed him in more meaningless ways until he could find his primary target, the only woman in his life who had actually stood up to him. He found Joyce Butts in one of the back offices and fired two shots, one into her chest and the other into her head, smirking all the while. She collapsed without a word, to his delight. She, too, survived. He may have been excellent at placing shots on a human-shaped target, but the human body itself is, luckily for Joyce, considerably more complex and resilient than paper.

He locked himself in one of the computer offices, where he found one of his old co-workers, a young woman by the name of Vicky Jackson, crouching on the floor. He dragged her to her feet and she braced herself for worse treatment to come, but calm had swept over Ronald now. All of the fire and fury drained out of him, and he set the gun down on the table beside him, even offering his backup pistol to her if it would help her to calm down. He gently told her to call the police, that he wasn't going to hurt her, and that it was all over now. After she had made the call he explained, 'I've come to do what I wanted to do. It's all over now. I've gotten everybody who wanted to hurt me.'

For the next few minutes, he made polite small-talk with Vicky Jackson, asking her about her Christmas and talking about the weather and people that they knew about town. He asked why she had never come to visit him when he worked in the Mini-Mart, and she told him that she had just missed his shifts when she happened to be in. He offered her a cigarette to calm her nerves and they both sat smoking companionably.

She was shaken by how normal he seemed after everything that he had just done. He was so calm that she even managed to get a little bit of information out of him before the police arrived. He had taken her hostage and arranged to be arrested in this way not because he was scared of death—in fact, he was absolutely certain that he would be killed for the things that he had done—but because he feared that in a shootout with the police he might end up paralysed or in a vegetative state. He had seen things like that happen to people back in his army days, and the thought of that complete loss of control absolutely haunted him. It would have been the complete antithesis of everything that he had worked towards his entire life. He knew that he was going to die, but that death was going to be on his own terms, with all of his work in this world done and all of the wrongs done against him avenged.

Part 5: Guilty as Charged

When the police arrived, Ronald Simmons was taken into custody without a single word. After he handed over his gun, he was searched and then loaded into a van for immediate transportation to the station. Ronald was booked at the Pope County Police Department. Before he ever saw the inside of a jail cell, all the other reports began filtering through. Simmons had only been arrested for the attempted murder of his former supervisor Joyce Butts so far. As he sat in the police station, the reports of all the other crimes in his spree began to come in. He would not speak to the police, but he would give a terse nod each time they asked him if he was the one responsible for a crime. Eventually the phone stopped ringing, the office returned to its usual state of silence, and Simmons' paperwork was processed.

The small-town police department could have coped with an angry employee shooting their boss—murder wasn't a common occurrence but it was at least something that they were mentally prepared to deal with. What Simmons had done was so far outside of their realm of experience that they couldn't even understand it. They were about to book him into the local jail when the death threats began to pour in, some of them more elaborate, some of them chillingly simple. It was clear that if he remained in Russellville, the town's tiny jail would come under attack and the man would be strung up in the middle of the night. They skipped ahead to the next logical step in their plans: they sent him to a mental hospital for evaluation, beyond of the easy reach of the enraged residents of the town who had just lost friends and family to his rampage. They used words like maniac, lunatic, and crazy to describe Ronald Gene Simmons, because they could not conceive of a world in which a sane man would kill the way that Simmons had killed. Without pity, mercy, or any discernible motive. If they thought that they had reached the ground floor of his depravity, they were in for more shocks.

A police escort drove Simmons south to the Arkansas State Hospital in Little Rock. The deputy, James Bolin, who would soon become Sheriff of the county, seemed to be the only one of the Pope police who recognised the reclusive man at all. He remembered that Simmons had a large family back at home and, considering the state that the man was in, he became concerned. He leaned in close and asked Ronald, 'You've got a family up there on Mockingbird Hill. Are they doing all right?'

Simmons maintained his stoic silence as he had been trained to do if he was ever captured by the enemy, but his lower lip quivered. Staring closely, Bolin thought that he could see a tear in the man's eye. It was enough of a sign for him to demand that the family be checked on immediately.

While Simmons was in the hospital, he was examined thoroughly over the course of three days by staff psychiatrist Dr Irving Kuo. Even as he spent his days with Simmons, Dr Kuo was still receiving regular reports from the police on Simmons' crimes as the evidence against the man mounted. First the bodies in town, then the bodies in the house, then the rest.

The police had prepared themselves for the worst, but their imaginations could not encompass all that they would find at Mockingbird Hill. After Deputy Bolin crept up to the house and took a peek in through the window, the local police immediately contacted their state counterparts for assistance. They had neither the experience nor the training to handle a massacre of this magnitude. It took both local and state troopers days of searching before they could recover all the bodies. The strange ways that Ronald had hidden some of them, laid others out, treated the corpses with kerosene, wrapped some in plastic and dispatched them with different methods confused the forensics teams to no end. The children wrapped in plastic were the last to be discovered, days after the rest of the family had already been sent off to the coroner's office to determine their causes of death for certain.

While there was plenty of physical evidence, there was no motive to be found anywhere. James Bolin led much of the local investigation and found that nobody really knew the Simmons family. Ronald's enforced solitude had precisely the desired effect. They had no family nearby who could be contacted. They had no friends, and even the people who they regularly interacted with, such as the owner of the gas station just down the road from Mockingbird Hill, said that Ronald would go about his business as though he was the only person in the world, never even bothering to speak during most visits to the store where he would purchase his cigarettes and beer almost daily.

Bolin was able to reconstruct a chronology of the events that took place, breaking down the murders into three clusters. He quickly came to the conclusion that to execute the murders with such precision, Ronald had to be a cunning and calculating man, but beyond that he could make no sense of the man's actions beyond his terrible temper. The vital details of Simmons family life would not surface for years after the case was closed.

In the end, despite Simmons complete refusal to cooperate with Dr Kuo, he was judged to be mentally competent to stand trial for his crimes on the basis that he knew the difference between life and death, and right and wrong. At the time, there was a strong belief among the police that he may have been mentally disabled in some way, and it was only years later, after criminologists had poured over the details of this case to create a timeline of events, that they realised just how accurate Bolin's initial assessment was and how fiercely intelligent Simmons needed to be to orchestrate the whole thing in such a way that none of his victims had a chance to escape.

Simmons was sent to prison, where details of his crimes were withheld from the general population of prisoners, for his safety, for as long as possible. It took less than a day for his story to finally hit the news cycle. Simmons had made local history by committing the single largest mass murder in all of Arkansas and national news for committing the worst crime involving a single family in US history. His claim to fame meant that the population of the prison held barely concealed loathing for him at best and murderous intent at worst. He was kept isolated for his own safety until his first trial.

His lawyers, Robert 'Doc' Irwin and John Harris, were public defenders assigned to his case, and despite his desire to plead guilty to everything and his outright loathing for them, they planned to make sure that his trials went as well as possible, given who their client was and what he had done. They argued that it would be impossible to find a jury that was not prejudiced if he was brought up on the two murder charges in Russellville after he had already been convicted of being a family annihilator, so the two cases were separated. They also worked diligently to quash hearsay and evidence from unrelated cases, such as his outstanding warrant for arrest for incest in New Mexico, that might turn a jury against him. Despite their frankly herculean work to turn the tide of opinion in Ronald Gene Simmons' favour, he was unrepentant and determined to plead guilty on every count, giving no justifications or excuses for his behaviour to the court that might have given them reason to doubt that he would kill again in an instant if given provocation. He received the death sentence by lethal injection for the murders in Russellville, in addition to 147 years in prison, and was transferred to Death Row.

The status of the death penalty in Arkansas at the time was a complex situation. It had only recently been made legal again after years of being banned. The laws that would later develop ensuring that every death penalty automatically ran the gamut of appeals through every court in the state had not even begun to materialise yet, and the complex meeting of public opinion on a contentious issue and the actual legal structure of the day was leading to many problems, entirely exacerbated when Ronald Gene Simmons refused to appeal his sentence, claiming that death was exactly what he deserved.

On death row, there were multiple attempts on Simmons' life. Not because of the terrible crimes that he had committed—he was surrounded by killers who were just as cold-blooded as him—but because they believed that his refusal to appeal his sentence would be used against them in their own appeals. There is a strange structure to the American legal system where every legal decision that is made can then be cited as a justification for any future decisions. This system, known as 'precedent', is why every judge is so careful before issuing a judgement and why so many styles of defence have been disallowed for fear of the way that they can be applied to other, unrelated cases. This system of living law allows for the constantly adjusting landscape of the modern world. Because there is no limitation on how far back a lawyer can reach for a case to cite, it can also lay undue weight on decisions that were made under what was essentially a completely different legal system.

In theory, this system pleases both the stoic conservatives who wish to stay close to the traditional understanding of the law and the more progressive lawyers who wish to lay down new interpretations. In practice, it means that a single bad decision made by a judge in the lower courts can have a lasting impact on the whole legal landscape, and that well-read lawyers can pull out legal precedent to justify practically any position or defence that they can come up with to suit whatever mood they believe that the jury is going to be in. In Arkansas, precedent was still being set for death penalty cases. The hope was that the state would adopt the policy of other states, where every appeal had to be exhausted before the death penalty could be enacted, but of course, someone like Ronald Gene Simmons threw a wrench in the works.

His second trial arrived shortly after the first. As he was pleading guilty and had no intention of raising a defence, the state did not feel the need to give his defenders much time to pull together a case. As in the first trial, the prosecutor was a district attorney by the name of John Bynum. Unlike the first trial, the case that he was trying to present to the jury did not come with a conveniently pre-packaged motive. Bynum was forced to scrape through all of the evidence that the police had collected from the Simmons estate, finally settling on one single piece of evidence, combined with some long-forgotten court documents from the family's time in Cloudcroft, New Mexico, in the family's safety deposit box in the bank in Russellville—communications between Ronald and his daughter Sheila that one or the other of them had held onto, either as blackmail material or out of sentimental value. Between that letter and the indictment for incest, Bynum was able to weave a narrative in which a sexually aggressive, incestuous rapist turned on his family when he was denied what he considered to be his 'rights'. Simmons worked with his lawyers for the first time in the entire proceedings in an attempt to get that letter blocked from entry into the evidence.

Bynum stood up in court in front of the jury and read every word from the private letters that Ronald had shared with his lover and daughter. The girl who had ruined his life. The girl who he blamed for everything. He had destroyed her and all evidence that they had ever been together. He had wrung the last trace of proof that they had ever been together out with his bare hands. Bynum was letting the whole world know. He was sharing all of Ronald's secrets. Ronald sat behind the bench glowering at the man through every carefully enunciated word of his own clumsy writing. He listened to his own confessions of love. He listened to Sheila reciprocating. He heard it all happening again. All of the things that he had killed her to stop. Bynum strolled past Ronald with the smug grin of a job well done.

Ronald didn't know that he could still get so angry that the world turned black until he was up out of his seat. His fist connected with the smug prick's jaw and sent him flying. Ronald clambered over the felled lawyer, ready to beat the man to death in full view of the whole court, when an officer of the court rushed over to stop him. Instinct took over. He snatched at the deputy's gun. It caught on the holster strap for the half second that it took the other officers of the court to arrive.

They dogpiled on top of him. Despite his screaming and struggling, they clapped him in chains and then dragged him out of the courtroom as he roared murderous threats at the fallen Bynum. Then the judge sent them off to decide Simmons' guilt.

He was convicted, with little deliberation, and sentenced to death by lethal injection, again once for each of his victims. In his final court appearance, he thanked the judge for his sentence, declaring that death was the only suitable justice for what he had done. Bynum, keeping his distance, seemed inordinately pleased with the results, too.

Almost immediately after the second trial, Simmons lawyers began working on appeals for him even though he had officially denied any wish to move forward with one. One of his lawyers moved to have Simmons judged incompetent to deny his right to appeal, going as far as to put himself forward as a legal guardian for the killer. This attempt was thwarted when it made its way to the Arkansas Supreme Court, using the same evaluation of Simmons that made it possible for him to stand trial to begin with. Dr Kuo's assessment stated that Simmons clearly understood the difference between life and death, which was all that the court felt was required. The legal process of ending Simmons' life kept on rolling forward, making national news once more after his outright refusal to raise an appeal against the order for his execution. Even Sheriff Bolin, who had seen the full nightmarish extent of Simmons' actions, felt the need to speak out against the death penalty, stating that despite the cunning that Simmons had displayed in setting up these killings, someone, as warped as him, shouldn't be making life and death decisions for all of the people in Arkansas.

*

In his cell, Ronald Gene Simmons was watching television and eating his last meal. The date for his execution had finally come, and he was facing it with all of the serene calm that characterised him when everything was going according to plan. He would die under the watchful eye of a doctor. They would make sure that he was completely gone before they buried him. There was no possibility of his being trapped inside his body with no means for escape. It was as clean an ending as he could have possibly hoped for, and he had no complaints. His life had been limited, but he had lived it in the way that he wanted to. Dying on his own terms was the natural conclusion of that.

Prison and military service both suited Ronald equally well, each of them filling up his days with carefully scheduled activities and allowing him to abdicate all responsibility for his actions. That lawyer had tried to dig up business that was meant to be left buried. It had been a near thing in that courtroom, but now it was over and he could set that worry aside. He would never step into a courtroom again for the rest of his life, even if the rest of his life could now be measured in minutes. He finished his meal, set the tray aside, and stared blankly at the television screen, laughing along with the laugh track, nodding along with the talking heads and doing his very best impression of looking like a perfectly normal human being. He wouldn't have to maintain any sort of charade for much longer, so the least that he could do was be comfortable.

He waited and listened for the time on the news before flicking the channel again. He aligned his internal clock with that and kept on counting. It wouldn't be long now. He didn't think that he would be afraid. He had never really believed that he would be afraid when the time finally came. That was why the war never scared him. That was why things in life never really scared him that made other men tremble in their boots. So long as he knew what was going to happen, he didn't have to worry about the all possibilities exploding out in every direction. Even if there was only a bad end to the road that he was on, he didn't mind so long as he knew which way he was going.

The time kept on ticking by. Any minute now the guards would come walking along to clap him in chains. They would lead him to the chamber, lay him down on the table, and slip that needle in his arm to take all of the pain and worry away. Once he was lying down on that table, he would never have to raise his weary head again. He waited until a full minute past the allotted time, then he wandered over to the bars of his cell to look as far down as he could. Where the hell were they?

The political firestorm around the death penalty continued as one of the other death row inmates filed a suit in Simmons defence, on the basis that Simmons' refusal of his right to appeal hurt the legal standing of the other prisoners who were fighting against their own sentencing. The Supreme Court tossed this defence out just as readily as they had the argument that Simmons wasn't competent to stand trial or the argument that his public defender knew what was best for him, but the legal machinations of denying that appeal had brought the planned execution to a grinding halt. Without the correct paperwork in hand, the governor was forced to call the prison a few minutes before the execution was meant to go ahead and order a stay until the situation in the Supreme Court was settled. The situation was eventually explained to Simmons, after he had already eaten his last meal, and he took the news with all of the grace with which he met any changes to his schedule—he was absolutely furious that someone was trying to interfere with his fate. His execution was rescheduled for a later date, and he was left locked in his cell once more with nothing more to occupy him than the endless loop of his thoughts.

On May 31st 1990, future president Bill Clinton, who was then serving as the Governor of Arkansas, signed Simmons' second death warrant, for June the 25th. This was the fastest pipeline from conviction to execution in United States history since the death penalty had been reinstated in 1976. Since the last trial, Simmons had habitually refused any visitors, and he did not break that pattern on the day of his execution, outright refusing a visit from either legal counsel or clergy. He was led into the room where he would be executed, where he loudly proclaimed, 'Justice delayed, finally be done, is justifiable homicide.'

It took 17 minutes for the doctor to declare that Ronald Gene Simmons was finally dead. The state held onto the body for the mandatory time, waiting for a family member to step forward and claim it, but there was nobody left. He was buried in a pauper's grave in Star City, Arkansas, far from the families of his victims and anyone who might have remembered his name.

In Pope County, Simmons was not so easily forgotten. His name is still spoken in hushed tones. He is the boogeyman of the small backwater towns of Arkansas, an evil so dark that adults can't even speak the names of his crimes. Earl Humphrey, the principal of the Dover Elementary School that Little Becky had attended said, 'We're trying to decide what we tell children, but I don't see any answers. I see a lot of adults with no answers. There's no way to explain this.'

In the days after Simmons' massacre, local psychologists were called out en masse to deal with the devastating impact that a crime like this can have on a town's psyche. They were sent out to the schools to console the children. Some of the victims, children of the killer, had attended the local school, and not one teacher had noticed that anything about their nightmarish home life was abnormal. The businesses that he had attacked were pillars of the Russellville community. The murderer himself had walked among them for years without ever raising an eyebrow, completely invisible and as indistinguishable from their fellow citizens as a wolf in sheep's clothing. As loathsome as it was, the whole of Arkansas had felt Ronald Gene Simmons' touch and wouldn't soon forget the experience. To this day, he still has the spurious honour of being Arkansas' most prolific mass murderer.

Part 6: Conclusion

We live in a chaotic world. For some, the constant state of flux is a source of joy and excitement, but for others it is the root of all fear. How we respond to the chaos is often what defines us. It is what separates the heroes from the bystanders, the downtrodden from the opportunists.

For many, exerting some control over the world is the only way that they can feel peace. They create a tiny universe of their own that they can predict and manage. All of us do this to a degree, seeking out familiar patterns and familiar faces, eating comfort food and building routines. For Simmons, control meant much more than taco Tuesdays or watching the same television show every week. It was his means of coping with a life that had been fraught with instability. If he had remained a solitary man, his life, despite his exemplary military record, would have disappeared into history. Simmons' need for perfect control and order in every part of his life made him into a tyrant to his family and to everyone else who had the misfortune to cross his path. He made his need for control into everyone else's problem, dictating every moment of their lives and lashing out fiercely when his orders were not obeyed.

Gradually, his need for control grew. With each new uncertainty that life brought, he tightened his grip on the things that were within his reach. At some point, this evolved beyond a defensive measure into a genuine passion. He took pleasure in dominating others. Exerting his power over his wife and children became a purpose unto itself.

If he were a man of limited intelligence, then his actions could be passed off as an inability to cope, and some of his more eccentric behaviour could have been written off as crime born of ignorance. But Simmons was not a stupid man. He excelled in his military career and held white-collar jobs competently until his personality problems drove him out of them. And he showed an ability to manipulate people, plan complex scenarios, and predict potential outcomes in a manner that only a true, highly intelligent, psychopath can.

Eventually, the inevitable happened. One of the people that Simmons thought that he controlled completely slipped their leash, and his perfectly ordered world began to come unravelled. People that he had dominated, mind and body, began thinking for themselves, making their own decisions and leaving him behind. He could not tolerate it.

Throughout his life, Simmons sought to close off any avenue of escape for his victims. He found ways to convince them that their only choice was to obey him, that his way was the only way. When manipulation, threats, and psychological warfare failed him, he did the only thing that he could to remove all other choices and possibilities from his victims' futures.

Ronald Gene Simmons has been labelled by the clinical psychologists who have examined his case as a textbook version of the 'control oriented psychopath'. According to them, everything that he did stemmed from this disorder, this inability to empathise with others or see them as more than just pieces in the games that he was playing. All that mattered to Simmons was maintaining control of every situation, no matter what the outcome of his control might be.

This diagnosis may gloss over many of Simmons' more interesting traits as a killer. For one thing, psychopaths are generally incapable of fear and appear confident in all social situations, while Simmons seemed to suffer from considerable anxiety over loss and failed to maintain relationships even when the power balance was tipped massively in his favour. Psychopaths who kill are characterised by their poor impulse control, while Simmons not only carefully planned and executed his massacre but also held down long-term jobs with only a few minor issues caused by his aggressive sexual advances. There is no denying that many of Simmons' actions could be explained away by a diagnosis of psychopathy, and for many that is a much more comforting thought than the idea that a perfectly sane man could commit crimes of this magnitude and brutality.

Whether he was too paralyzed by fear to allow anyone else their freedom or he was a cold-blooded psychopath who derived pleasure from forcing his will on others, the result was the same. He made the lives of his family into a living hell and then he took even that living hell from them in an orgy of violence, just because his daughter refused to reciprocate his deviant sexual advances anymore.

In the end, Simmons' murderous rampage claimed sixteen of the twenty people he attacked. Of those sixteen, only two were not members of his family, although in a community as tightly knit as that in Russellville and Dover, almost everyone is as close as family to everyone else.

Simmons' crimes were planned out meticulously and committed over the course of a few days starting just before Christmas, 1987 but the life that led him to that moment, the turns of fate that shaped the man into not just a killer but a family annihilator, started decades before when a boy lost his father and was plunged into chaos.

Want More?

Did you enjoy *Obeying Evil* and want some more True Crime?

YOUR FREE BOOK IS WAITING

From bestselling author Ryan Green

There is a man who is officially classed as **"Britain's most dangerous prisoner"**

The man's name is Robert Maudsley, and his crimes earned him the nickname **"Hannibal the Cannibal"**

This free book is an exploration of his story...

amazonkindle **nook** **kobo** **iBooks**

 *"Ryan brings the horrifying details to life. I can't wait to read more by this author!"*

Get a free copy of ***Robert Maudsley: Hannibal the Cannibal*** when you sign up to join my Reader's Group.

www.ryangreenbooks.com/free-book

Every Review Helps

If you enjoyed the book and have a moment to spare, I would really appreciate a short review on Amazon. Your help in spreading the word is gratefully received and reviews make a huge difference to helping new readers find me. Without reviewers, us self-published authors would have a hard time!

Type in your link below to be taken straight to my book review page.

US   geni.us/OEUS

UK   geni.us/OEUK

Australia geni.us/OEAUS

Canada   geni.us/OECA

Thank you! I can't wait to read your thoughts.

About Ryan Green

Ryan Green is a true crime author who lives in Herefordshire, England with his wife, three children, and two dogs. Outside of writing and spending time with his family, Ryan enjoys walking, reading and windsurfing.

Ryan is fascinated with History, Psychology and True Crime. In 2015, he finally started researching and writing his own work and at the end of the year, he released his first book on Britain's most notorious serial killer, Harold Shipman.

He has since written several books on lesser-known subjects, and taken the unique approach of writing from the killer's perspective. He narrates some of the most chilling scenes you'll encounter in the True Crime genre.

You can sign up to Ryan's newsletter to receive a free book, updates, and the latest releases at:

WWW.RYANGREENBOOKS.COM

More Books by Ryan Green

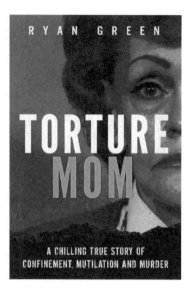

In July 1965, teenagers Sylvia and Jenny Likens were left in the temporary care of Gertrude Baniszewski, a middle-aged single mother and her seven children.

The Baniszewski household was overrun with children. There were few rules and ample freedom. Sadly, the environment created a dangerous hierarchy of social Darwinism where the strong preyed on the weak.

What transpired in the following three months was both riveting and chilling. The case shocked the entire nation and would later be described as "The single worst crime perpetuated against an individual in Indiana's history".

More Books by Ryan Green

On 29th February 2000, John Price took out a restraining order against his girlfriend, Katherine Knight. Later that day, he told his co-workers that she had stabbed him and if he were ever to go missing, it was because Knight had killed him.

The next day, Price didn't show up for work.

A co-worker was sent to check on him. They found a bloody handprint by the front door and they immediately contacted the police. The local police force was not prepared for the chilling scene they were about to encounter.

Price's body was found in a chair, legs crossed, with a bottle of lemonade under his arm. He'd been decapitated and skinned. The "skin-suit" was hanging from a meat hook in the living room and his head was found in the kitchen, in a pot of vegetables that was still warm. There were two plates on the dining table, each had the name of one of Price's children on it.

She was attempting to serve his body parts to his children.

More Books by Ryan Green

In 1902, at the age of 11, Carl Panzram broke into a neighbour's home and stole some apples, a pie, and a revolver. As a frequent troublemaker, the court decided to make an example of him and placed him into the care of the Minnesota State Reform School. During his two-year detention, Carl was repeatedly beaten, tortured, humiliated and raped by the school staff.

At 15-years old, Carl enlisted in the army by lying about his age but his career was short-lived. He was dishonourably discharged for stealing army supplies and was sent to military prison. The brutal prison system sculpted Carl into the man that he would remain for the rest of his life. He hated the whole of mankind and wanted revenge.

When Carl left prison in 1910, he set out to rob, burn, rape and kill as many people as he could, for as long as he could. His campaign of terror could finally begin and nothing could stand in his way.

More Books by Ryan Green

In 1861, the police of a rural French village tore their way into the woodside home of Martin Dumollard. Inside, they found chaos. Paths had been carved through mounds of bloodstained clothing, reaching as high as the ceiling in some places.

The officers assumed that the mysterious maid-robber had killed one woman but failed in his other attempts. Yet, it was becoming sickeningly clear that there was a vast gulf between the crimes they were aware of and the ones that had truly been committed.

Would Dumollard's wife expose his dark secret or was she inextricably linked to the atrocities? Whatever the circumstances, everyone was desperate to discover whether the bloody garments belonged to some of the 648 missing women.

Free True Crime Audiobook

Sign up to Audible and use your free credit to download this collection of twelve books. If you cancel within 30 days, there's no charge!

WWW.RYANGREENBOOKS.COM/FREE-AUDIOBOOK

"Ryan Green has produced another excellent book and belongs at the top with true crime writers such as M. William Phelps, Gregg Olsen and Ann Rule" –**B.S. Reid**

"Wow! Chilling, shocking and totally riveting! I'm not going to sleep well after listening to this but the narration was fantastic. Crazy story but highly recommend for any true crime lover!" –**Mandy**

"Torture Mom by Ryan Green left me pretty speechless. The fact that it's a true story is just…wow" –**JStep**

"Graphic, upsetting, but superbly read and written" –**Ray C**

WWW.RYANGREENBOOKS.COM/FREE-AUDIOBOOK

Made in United States
Troutdale, OR
03/05/2024

18239457R00056